Supervising Psychotherapy

Supervising Psychotherapy

Psychoanalytic and Psychodynamic Perspectives

Edited by
Christine Driver and Edward Martin

Contributors
Mary Banks, Christine Driver, Gertrud Mander,
Edward Martin, John Stewart

SAGE Publications
London • Thousand Oaks • New Delhi

SAGE Publications Ltd
6 Bonhill Street
London EC2A 4PU

SAGE Publications Inc
2455 Teller Road
Thousand Oaks, California 91320

SAGE Publications India Pvt Ltd
32, M-Block Market
Greater Kailash – I
New Delhi 110 048

British Library Cataloguing in Publication data

A catalogue record for this book is
available from the British Library

ISBN 0 7619 6870 9
ISBN 0 7619 6871 7 (pbk)

Library of Congress Control Number available

Typeset by Line Arts, Pondicherry, India.
Printed and bound in Great Britain by Anthenaeum Press, Gateshead

*To Happy Associations
with Creative Colleagues*

Contents

Notes on Authors

Mary Banks is a Member of the British Association of Psychotherapists having originally trained as a Counsellor at Birkbeck College.

Christine Driver is a Member of the Society of Analytical Psychology and a Psychotherapy member of FPC, having originally trained as a Counsellor with WPF Counselling and Psychotherapy.

Gertrud Mander is a Psychotherapy member of FPC having originally trained as a Counsellor at WPF Counselling and Psychotherapy, and is an author of a number of books and papers.

Edward Martin is a Member of the Society of Analytical Psychology having originally trained as a marital counsellor with London Marriage Guidance.

John Stewart is a Psychotherapy Member of FPC having originally trained as a Counsellor with WPF Counselling and Psychotherapy.

All are or have been involved as trainers, supervisors, external examiners and seminar leaders with WPF Counselling and Psychotherapy Training in Supervision in London and provincial centres. All are members of the British Association for Psychoanalytic and Psychodynamic Supervision.

Foreword

I am very pleased to welcome a book on supervision from a psychoanalytic perspective. This book has been written by people who designed and taught on the supervision training at WPF Counselling and Psychotherapy, one of the first places in the UK to recognise the importance of supervision as a discipline in its own right. The history of the concept of supervision as such is well known. It has developed out of the early methods of training psychoanalysts and analytical psychologists although it is now recognised as essential for all who use talking therapies.

Originally, the training analyst also supervised the training cases of their analysands. In the UK, it was not until 1947 that the Institute of Psychoanalysis decided that there should be a second analyst to supervise the candidate's work. Reasons for this were that the analyst had to become more 'real' in order to teach and work with the supervisee's work with patients. There might also be a strong tendency to idealise the analyst as a 'wise master' of the craft. There were still at that time several eminent analysts who did not agree, objecting on the grounds that the candidate's counter transferences could best be understood by the candidate's own analyst.

Even when supervision had become clearly separated from analysis as a distinct activity in its own right, there was still a long way to go before supervision would be a discipline, studied, taught and practised with recognition of all the complexity that it entails. Analysts to begin with merely followed their instincts. Some conducted supervision exactly like analysis. They might have been silent and withholding, interpreting when moved to do so. This sort of supervision would give little opportunity for exploration, discussion or debate and missed the magnificent opportunity to discover the dynamics of the supervisory relationship and its resonance with the therapeutic relationship.

Now the discipline is coming of age. This book is a distillation of the thinking and learning that has taken place from all the experiences of analytic supervision during the second half of the twentieth century. Its usefulness is clear. The British Association for Counselling and Psychotherapy has always firmly decreed that all counsellors must be supervised whenever they are working. Sue Wheeler (*Counselling*, 2000) made clear that although there is a great demand for supervision, there is also a shortage of well trained supervisors. New courses to train supervisors have been set up but as Sue Wheeler (2000) points out, there has been some uncertainty about what should constitute the curriculum for such training. This book should provide a useful text for any training course that covers the dynamic aspects of the supervisory relationship, which can be discovered and structured by an understanding of analytic theory in its broadest sense.

Although counsellors are clearly convinced of the value and importance of supervision, psychotherapists have tended to consider that after training was completed, supervision became optional and as one became more senior in the profession, it could be dispensed with completely. Guggenbuhl Craig (1971) famously described the difficulties of the senior therapist or analyst who cannot go to anyone for supervision, because he either knows everybody or is senior to them. This argument implies a teacher–pupil model of supervision and this book does much to point out that supervision may be a very different process of exploration in which both halves of the couple are engaged in discovering how the client will affect what happens between them as well as what happens in the therapy sessions.

The national regulating bodies for psychotherapy (e.g. The United Kingdom Council for Psychotherapy (UKCP) and British Confederation for Psychotherapy (BCP)) do not currently register supervisors. The British Association for Counselling and Psychotherapy on the other hand does accredit supervisors. UKCP is currently considering registration for supervisors and will engage in a debate about the necessity for compulsory supervision or consultation. At the moment it is still a matter for each psychotherapist to decide for him or herself. Whatever happens in the future in terms of regulation, this book will give food for thought, particularly for those who work analytically although it should be useful for anyone who is aware that more happens in human interactions than can be accounted for by common sense. In other words, there is room for a concept of depth and of patterns of behaviour, thought and feeling that are not immediately obvious at first sight.

Lesley Murdin
Head of Training, WPF Counselling and Psychotherapy

References

Guggenbuhl Craig, A. (1971) *Power in the Helping Professions* Dallas, TX: Spring.
Wheeler, S. (2000) 'Supervision', *Counselling*, September 2000.

Acknowledgements

This book has taken several years to gestate and write and the authors would like to thank all their families and friends for their support and encouragement. In addition we would like to thank all the supervisees, supervisors and colleagues who have enabled us to creatively consider the supervisory processes, and WPF Counselling and Psychotherapy for their commitment to the exploration and study of supervision. The bringing together of this experience by the supervisory team of the authors has enabled this book to emerge.

Introduction: Orientation and Themes

Christine Driver

Orientation

When someone becomes a supervisor it is usually from a position of having become established as a psychotherapist or counsellor. They have trained, they have been in supervision, and they are familiar with the intimate world of working with a patient or client and the sometimes intense transference and counter-transference issues that emerge from within the therapeutic dyad. It is perhaps easy to assume that familiarity and experience of working as a therapist provides the expertise to supervise others who are doing the same. It is, therefore, often surprising to discover the multitude of tasks and internal places that the supervisor needs to occupy and work within to work effectively with the unconscious processes that are thrown up within the clinical rhombus (Ekstein and Wallerstein, 1972).

Like the commencement of therapy or supervision this introduction outlines the content of the book and the issues which are covered. It sets a contract between the writers and the reader as to the nature of the book and with it, introduces the nature of the supervisory processes which we are exploring. The authors have all trained in supervision and work as supervisors and have been involved with the training of supervisors on the Diploma in Supervision run by WPF Counselling and Psychotherapy, one of the first organisations to run training courses in supervision in the UK. They are therefore familiar, from first hand experience, with the complexities of the task, and the issues and anxieties that supervision evokes. Supervision is a relationship based on the need to understand another, the patient. What is created in supervision is a representation of the patient through the communications of the supervisee. Therefore for the supervisor the patient is an imaginary figure, experienced through the communications (conscious and unconscious) of the supervisee. Therapists need theoretical constructs and frameworks in order to make sense of the patient and the impact of unconscious communications. Similarly, supervisors need a theoretical underpinning and an analytic attitude to enable their supervisees to develop their understanding of the patient. The underlying philosophy of all the authors is that understanding is gained by processing experience, which leads to the development of an 'observing ego' that can hold and juggle the triangular nature of supervision and the supervisory processes to make conscious the unconscious identifications and communications within it. Although all the writers have different styles and different foci we all approach supervision from the standpoint that it is through the accessing of unconscious processes and counter-transference phenomenon within supervision that the therapeutic work with the client is developed.

The supervisory task is complex because it requires an understanding of the external and internal dynamics of many relationships. For example, the client and the therapist, the therapist and the supervisor, the supervisor and the organisation, the organisation and the supervisor, the supervisor and the therapist, the therapist and the client. Each of these relationships has internal and external dynamics operating simultaneously at conscious and unconscious levels. The supervisor needs to hold and try to unravel these within the supervisory process. Supervisors therefore need to do a lot of decoding and unravelling of the conscious and unconscious dynamics so that the dynamics can be understood in relation to the clinical work and the development of the supervisee. Without supervision we would all get stuck with our 'blind spots', 'defensive avoidance of certain information', due to the supervisee's pathology (Szecsödy, 1990: 250) and 'dumb spots', 'lack of knowledge, information and skill' (Szecsödy, 1990: 250) and be in danger of enacting something by inappropriate didactic comments or interpretations, or oversight of unconscious communications rather than creating understanding within the supervisee about the patient.

Perhaps one of the major internal shifts a supervisor needs to make is to be able to accommodate, consider, juggle and challenge the variety of foci which supervision entails. Alongside this supervisors need to develop their authority in relation to these foci, and the issues they present, so as to consider and confront them internally and externally. Therapeutic 'authority' comes from the therapist's ability to make sense of the internal world of the patient and the way the patient relates from this to the external world. Supervisory 'authority' comes from being able to simultaneously understand the needs and clinical issues of the patient, the learning needs of the supervisee, and the impact and limitations of the institution in which supervision takes place. Finding the authority to speak to these issues is perhaps one of the major tasks for the developing supervisor, but as Mattinson says, the supervisor also needs to consider, 'when to go in, and when to persist; and when to stay quietly by and allow the satisfaction the worker is obtaining in a twosome with the client' (1981: 18). The supervisor therefore needs to understand the nature of therapeutic processes as well as understanding how people learn so as to enable the supervisees to develop their own understanding of the patient and therapeutic work.

The developing awareness of the complexities of the supervisory task are evidenced in the increasing number of books and papers written on the subject over the past ten years. As practitioners have begun to think about the task and have become increasingly involved in this growing branch of the therapeutic profession there has been a realisation of the varied dynamics within which we work. When therapy was in its infancy the practitioners worked mainly on a one-to-one basis, which supervision reflected. The development of an awareness of the supervisory task has come through the ongoing development of therapeutic work in a range of settings. Ekstein and Wallerstein (1972) developed the concept of the parallel process and Mattinson (1975), in her early work on supervising social workers, built on Searles's (1986) ideas of the reflection process. The rise in voluntary counselling agencies and the consequent requirement of supervision, the expansion of the charitable and voluntary sector agencies such as Childline and Cruse, and the needs and requirements of supervision through the ongoing professionalisation prompted by the BACP and other networks has further developed this awareness. The growth in supervisory activity has brought supervision to the surface and an understanding that it requires something more than just being a therapist. It has also brought a growing realisation that the supervisory relationship is not just a dyad of one 'teaching' the other but is a triadic relationship in which the unconscious patterns of the clinical work are reflected in the supervisory process and that understanding evolves through its unravelling.

The book's overarching theme is the nature of supervision as a mutative process that enables the therapeutic development of the clinical work. A process that enables learning at an emotional, as well as at a cognitive, level. A process that is not therapy but nevertheless needs to be therapeutic. To do this supervisors have to develop an awareness of the many strands of the supervisory process and the chapters in this book aim to address the range of issues which are thrown up by working as a supervisor.

Themes

The supervisory relationship – external and internal dimensions

The first section of the book considers the various intrapersonal and interpersonal dynamics in the supervisory relationship, in the processes of supervision and in being a supervisor. Chapter 1 begins by examining how disparate trends in the history of supervision affect the work of supervision today. The history of psychodynamic therapy points to an early divergence of opinion concerning the method of training therapists through supervision. One model favoured the integration of supervision within the trainee's personal analysis. The other separated the trainee's analysis, appointing a second analyst to teach through a supervisory analysis. Later, a third model emerged that focused on supervision as the principal training method. Edward Martin explores how, despite the acceptance that psychodynamic therapy affects both patient and therapist, supervision tended to exclude the dynamics between supervisee and supervisor. The supervisee brings two communications to supervision; one from the patient, the other from themselves. The chapter discusses whether learning is optimised by concentrating supervision on the patient/supervisee dyad, or by responding to the unconscious communication between supervisee and supervisor. The relative informational value of fact and fantasy in supervision is discussed and the therapeutic and educational aspects of the supervisory role, constantly mobile within the triangular dynamic involving supervisor, supervisee and patient, are re-evaluated. The move from therapist to supervisor means working within a triangular relationship. The chapter focuses on how the fractal patterns of patient and therapist reverberate within the supervisory process and that it is the supervisor's task to work with these processes to enable supervision to be a mutative experience for the therapist in relation to their work with the patient.

Moving on from the history of supervision and the ramifications of triangular dynamics, Mary Banks, in Chapter 2, explores the internal and personal dimensions that are common to all therapists, and hence supervisors, and considers how the transition from therapist to supervisor is made and what this involves. She considers how it is the intrinsic impulse to heal that creates the jumping-off point for all healers and therapists. Her chapter emerges from her original research into the type of personality that becomes a therapist. Her findings suggest a healing type, a wounded healer with an impulse to heal, a phenomena which links ancestral healers with modern day therapists, mental health workers, etc. It is important to recognise that we become therapists as a result of, and with our, personal baggage. It is the way in which we develop and integrate this 'baggage' through therapy and training that forms us as therapists and from this our starting point in our development as supervisors. Mary Banks's chapter develops her thesis that practice is based on a combination of the healing personality with a theoretical perspective and that it is only with a combination of the two that healing happens. Theory without the personal is sterile, but the personal without an acknowledgement of limitations and insight is equally sterile. As we become supervisors we have to be aware of ourselves, use our personalities creatively and with insight and understanding. We come to being supervisors from the underlying basis of our wounded 'humanness' combined with the framework of theory, therapy and clinical experience and are hopefully able to hold the tensions of autonomy and humility within the supervisory relationship.

Recognising what we bring to supervision in terms of our personal and professional 'baggage' is important as we go on to consider what it is that we are doing in supervision. What do we need to consider and how do we need to 'be' to enable therapeutic supervision? Gertrud Mander considers this in Chapter 3. She focuses on supervision as an activity of 'thinking about thinking', of influencing and enabling supervisees to learn from experience and to develop a professional self with the help of sensitive supervisory attunement. She considers the need to carefully avoid the twin dangers of collusion with, and controlling of, the supervisee. She discusses how the 'good supervisor' encourages supervisees to model themselves on supervisory exploration by the supervisor rather than becoming supervisory clones who need certainties and need to get things right. Mander looks at training supervision as well as consultative supervision with experienced colleagues and emphasises the supervisor's role as a transformative object in a relationship that facilitates the emergence of a core professional self, and the establishment of competence and confidence. This enables the supervisee to do creative work within a well-functioning therapeutic relationship that contains the patient's anxieties as well as being a safe environment. Issues of assessment and of resistance from all three participants in the supervisory encounter are also addressed as are the complex parallel processes which arise unconsciously within the supervisory triad.

What is pertinent to any supervisory process, whether it be individual supervision or within a group, is a consideration of the dynamic processes that occur between the supervisor and the supervisee and in Chapter 4 Christine Driver goes on to consider these interactional dynamics. From the historical development of supervision came a certain *modus operandi* that tended to distance itself from the interactive processes between supervisor and supervisee. Searles (1986) brought this back into focus with his explorations into the reflection process and this chapter investigates how, within the frame of supervision, the process of supervision is experienced at various levels within the internal world of the supervisee and supervisor. The development of the clinical work of the supervisee occurs within the relationship between the supervisor and supervisee and through external and internal dialogue. However, transference and counter-transference inevitably affect the relationship and may reverberate with the clinical material. This chapter considers ways in which these issues can be understood and ways in which the dynamic interaction between the professional and personal self (Ekstein and Wallerstein, 1972) of the supervisee can generate change.

Learning in supervision

One of the aims of supervision is to enable learning, and learning in supervision involves emotional, mutative and therapeutic processes that enable the supervisee to conceptualise within the framework of the material that they are experiencing from their patients. John Stewart addresses this complex task in Chapter 5. He begins by considering how supervision can be defined and particular reference is made to the way in which the supervisory relationship constellates into a double triangular interface. He explores the link between supervision and styles of teaching and from this an examination of supervision as a theatre of learning is developed. Reference is made to recent research into the physical basis of learning from infancy onwards, and in particular, the ways in which memory develops. He then goes on to consider how this research can be linked and related to patterns of learning in the supervisory setting. One factor which does affect learning is anxiety and he goes on to examine the manner in which anxiety gives rise to psychological defence mechanisms and the ways in which such mechanisms may inhibit the capacity to learn. The concept of the learning position is examined in the light of the supervisory task and particular reference is made to supervision and learning within a training setting. In relation to this, and supervision generally, John Stewart considers variations between cognitive styles and the need to be aware of such variations in the learning styles of individual supervisees. The overall focus of the chapter is 'how do supervisees learn?' and in relation to this he goes on to consider the distinction between accommodative and assimilative learning, and the way this links to Winnicott's (1971) thinking about the location of cultural experience, in an attempt to consider the integration and application of theoretical constructs into the learning and practice of supervision and psychotherapy.

The setting and supervision

Organisations which offer psychotherapy and counselling make demands on the processes of the clinical work through the frameworks they require and they frequently need specialisms such as short-term therapy or the supervision of individual work in a group setting. In this section the authors look at the way these structures affect the processes of supervision and how supervisors can work with them.

Organisations often engage supervisors for group supervision for economic reasons but there are other riches to be gained from this necessity. Group supervision creates its own dynamics which are integral to and a valuable part of the supervisory process. A group provides a landscape onto which the clinical material settles and in which the dynamics of the group are affected. Christine Driver in Chapter 6 uses the metaphors of geography and topography to examine the dynamics of group supervision. It is a process which requires the supervisor to balance the basic modes of supervisory activity within the context and functions of a group. The chapter explores how good clinical practice and counsellor/therapist development can be facilitated through the experience and dynamics of group supervision. It illustrates the importance and significance of the interactional elements within the group, and the learning and understanding which can develop from these, in relation to understanding the clinical work with the patient.

Just as being a supervisor requires the ability to juggle a multitude of tasks so too does the organisational context and framework in which supervision takes place. One particular area in which clinical work has developed is the provision of counselling in workplace and organisational settings which often is based on short-term, focused, work. The workplace is therefore demanding that therapists use multiple skills. For instance many therapists requiring supervision, work in organisations that are engaged solely in various time-limited therapies. In Chapter 7 Gertrud Mander provides an exploration of the relationship between short-term therapy and the dynamics involved in its supervision. The brief psychotherapy model developed by Balint (1973) and Malan (1963) is extended to create a model of supervision needed for this task which has to encompass issues of assessment, structuring, focusing, ending and loss, all having to be dealt with in a short and concise framework which mirrors the therapeutic work.

Organisations add to (and subtract from) the dynamic of supervision in a variety of ways and in Chapter 8 John Stewart focuses on the interface between the process of supervision and the organisational context in which it exists. The chapter begins by giving a general introduction to the theme via a vignette that illustrates an organisational interaction which impinges upon the activity of supervision. This vignette is used to illustrate the points under consideration and the discussion is started by looking at ways in which we can think about organisations and how they manage their level of functioning and definition of roles in the service of their perceived tasks. To facilitate our understanding of this John Stewart uses two paradigms: that of an organism as an open and a closed system, and of it being analogous to that of the psychodynamic understanding of the human psyche. These models are linked to the supervisory process to develop the theme of this chapter, and the notion of the clinical rhombus, as developed by Ekstein and Wallerstein (1972), is used to amplify the link between organisational and supervisory processes. These ideas are extended, by the use of the triangle of involvement, to include the organisational issues the participants in the rhombus bring from their past and from current organisational involvement outside of the supervisory situation. The chapter then returns to the analogy of the psychodynamic understanding of the human psyche to consider ways in which unconscious processes manifest themselves through the ways in which organisations operate. Particular reference is made to the Kleinian concept of the paranoid–schizoid position, as a defence against anxiety, and movement towards the depressive position. John Stewart adapts the 'depressive position' to form the concept of a 'functioning position' within an organisational structure and relates this specifically to the process of supervision. He goes on to use Bion's formulations about the dichotomy between a functioning work group and the formation of basic assumption groups as a defence against anxiety, in relation to the organisational setting of supervision. One aspect of organisations that he considers is the manner in which client groups 'project into' the organisation and the necessity to understand this process so as to avoid a level of contamination which skews the functioning of the organisation and hence supervision. Supervisors have an important role to play in maintaining a healthy level of functioning in the organisations in which they supervise and they also have an obligation to support the work of the supervisee. John Stewart's chapter addresses the need for the supervisor to think carefully as to how to hold the organsational dimension in a way which protects the supervisory space from excessive intrusion.

Generic issues in supervision

Psychodynamic supervision is cognisant of the triangular relationship between patient, supervisor and supervisee and of the reflection process, in which patient material is reflected in the dynamic between the supervisor and supervisee. These are mainly unconscious processes, which therefore have to be interpreted. However, underlying all good supervision is good ethical practice. The earliest code of ethics for supervisors laid responsibility for selecting work for supervision with the supervisee. While this ensured clarity over where ultimate clinical responsibility lay, it meant that supervisors had to rely on the integrity of their supervisee as to what they presented in supervision and the way in which they used and valued their counter-transference. However, supervision effectively breaks the strict confidentiality which is assumed to exist between therapist and patient. In Chapter 9 Edward Martin considers the complex dynamics of confidentiality and other ethical dilemmas in supervision. He reflects on how codes of ethics are designed to protect the theft of inner world drama by the stronger (therapists) from the more vulnerable (patients). Martin suggests that this issue should be extended to include supervisors and supervisees (trained and trainee therapists), and he draws examples from the existing codes of ethics for supervisors. The chapter offers examples of what might be considered 'petty theft' or 'grand larceny' as well as the grey areas. One of these grey areas concerns confidentiality and there is a discussion about whether presenting a case for supervision breaches any strict interpretation of confidentiality and Martin asks what is the price paid for this breach.

Clinical work and supervision are always dealing with boundary issues and one needs to consider whether any therapy or analytic training automatically qualifies the trained therapist/analyst to supervise and whether supervisors always have 'blind spots'. Do supervisors always have aspects of their work that they are unable to visualise or speak to? If supervision is really to enable the therapist to enable the patient to 'think the unthinkable' then perhaps some form of supervision of supervisors is always required. Gertrud Mander, asks in Chapter 10 'how much is enough?'. In considering the supervision of supervision she is also addressing the issues of timing and endings in supervision. In therapy and in supervision these issues are similar and yet different in that more relationships are involved in supervising – the therapeutic couple, the supervisory couple and the three person dynamics, are all under constant observation. A third person, the patient, who is absent and yet the object of the activity, needs to be considered in all matters of timing and ending and this factor alters and complicates the process significantly, requiring a number of skills that supervisors need to adopt.

Chapter 11 begins by looking at timing in three ways: time as horizontal, i.e., length and duration of supervision contracts; time as vertical, i.e., time and timing in the supervisory session of interventions, format and frame issues; and the role of memory in supervision. This exploration is followed by a discussion of how and why the ending of supervision is different from therapy and how the presence of patients complicates the matter, i.e., whether the patients carry on with the supervisee (who may move on to another supervisor) or finish at the same time as the supervisee. The ending may be planned or unplanned, too early or too late, and there are always powerful issues of attachment, separation and loss which need to be addressed. Another important issue is the situation in which the ending is decided by the supervisor where, after careful assessment, the therapist's work is no longer considered satisfactory. Then the supervisee has to be sensitively enabled to stop, which can be a very difficult and not always a mutual decision. In whatever way an ending in supervision is reached it is always important that the ending be experienced as an act of professional integrity rather than as a sadistic exclusion from practising a desired profession.

Conclusion

It would be inappropriate and very uncreative to claim that all the authors totally endorse each other's points of view; thank goodness for difference! However the main thrust of the philosophy contained in these chapters is that supervision should itself be therapeutic. This apparently obvious statement is made because of the many anecdotal examples given in which supervisees describe their supervision as anything other than therapeutic. Therapeutic means that the work should engage the inner worlds of the supervisor, supervisee and the patient. Supervisors should also be aware that it is in supervision that supervisees become peculiarly vulnerable and regressed, to a lesser extent than therapeutic regression, but none the less a regressive transference is created between the supervisee and supervisor. The supervisor therefore needs to work with that knowledge and hold in awareness the interactive dynamics of all the factors affecting the supervisory process and hence the supervisee. Supervision which does not actively address the regressed pairing faces the potential danger that the supervisee will experience the supervisor merely as an intrusive, and at times a tyrannical, other. If supervision is to be effective the supervisor has to engage with the supervisee's unconscious, but in such a manner that the Oedipal triangle is not forgotten. In this way supervision can be therapeutic without being therapy and there is less likelihood of the supervisor being seduced into an incestuous relationship with the supervisee. Overall then, the aim of supervision is to hold, understand and work with the dynamics in a way that processes the experience in the service of the patient but also in a way that is mutative and enables the supervisee to learn and develop their therapeutic abilities.

The conclusion of the book deals with the ending of supervision and like any ending you may well be left with questions unanswered and issues unfinished. Our aim however is to raise questions and issues in your mind. Supervision is an active process, learning can never be passive because in understanding the nature of intra-and inter-personal relationships and intra-and inter-psychic relationships we have to actively engage with our own inner worlds, as both therapists and supervisors, to enable a mutative and therapeutic understanding of the patient and the material they present. Supervision is, in a very real sense, an arena of 'multi-tasking' within the framework of an analytic attitude. This is the thread which links all the authors of this book as they explore the various threads and dimensions of supervision. Supervision is a complex task, not just an extension of therapy, and its creativity as a process lies in our ability to begin to acknowledge and struggle with just this particular complexity.

Authors' note

The words 'patient' and 'client' are used interchangeably in this book according to the context in which the supervision takes place.

WPF Counselling and Psychotherapy (formerly Westminster Pastoral Foundation).

References

Balint, M. (1973) *Focal Psychotherapy, An Example of Applied Psychoanalysis*. London: Tavistock Publications.
Casement, P. (1985) *On Learning From The Patient*. London: Tavistock Publications.
Ekstein, R. and Wallerstein, R. (1972) *The Teaching and Learning of Psychotherapy*. Madison, CT: International Universities Press, Inc.
Malan D.H. (1963) *A Study of Brief Psychotherapy*. London: Tavistock Publications.
Mattinson, J. (1975) *The Reflection Process in Casework Supervision*. London: Tavistock Institute.
Mattinson, J. (1981) *The Deadly Equal Triangle*. Northampton, MA and London: The Smith College School of Social Work and the Group of the Advancement of Psychotherapy in Social Work.
Searles, H.F. (1986) *Collected Papers on Schizophrenia and Related Subjects*. London: Maresfield Library.
Szecsödy, I. (1990) 'Supervision: a didactic or mutative situation', *Psychoanalytic Psychotherapy*, 4(3): 245–64.
Winnicott, D. (1971) 'The Location of Cultural Experience' in D. Winnicott, *Playing and Reality*, pp. 112–21. London: Tavistock Publications.

PART I

THE SUPERVISORY RELATIONSHIP: EXTERNAL AND INTERNAL DIMENSIONS

Chapter 1

Listening to the Absent Patient: Therapeutic Aspects of Supervision

Edward Martin

The experience of an analytic relationship through personal analysis has always been the bedrock of the profession of analysis. As analytic training became more formalised a supervisory, or control analysis became an additional requirement. This development followed the pattern of medical training, with professional skills acquired through work discussions with a senior colleague. Who this more senior colleague should be became an issue for debate, with conflicting ideas emerging from Hungary and Austria.

The Hungarians favoured the control analysis being carried out by the trainee's own analyst. When trainees began treating their own patients, their analysis would include thoughts, feelings and fantasies about their patients. In this model, the link between the unconscious of the trainees and that of their patients was held only by their analysts. By contrast, the Viennese school held that the trainee's analysts should not 'control' the analytic work. In this second model, trainees were thought to benefit from exposure to a different clinical perspective and their work was therefore controlled by another analyst who would teach rather than analyse.

While the early form of analysis for trainees was didactic in character it later became clearly recognised that in order to work safely with patients, trainee analysts would themselves need a thorough therapeutic analysis and this became the norm. As far as supervision went the Viennese practice of separating the task of analyst and supervisor became the norm, and the

Hungarian model faded into the background. This structure has in turn influenced much of the training of therapists and psychodynamic counsellors.

With the Viennese model there is a grey area between therapy and supervision. The subjectivity of analyst and supervisor sometimes becomes persecutory for the trainee therapist who may, on the suggestion or even instruction of the supervisor, take material from supervision to therapy only to hear from the therapist that what has been taken is actually a supervisory matter. Another consequence of adopting the Viennese model is that qualified therapists eventually end their therapy. The therapist may continue working creatively until something is touched on which resonates with personal material that has not been worked through sufficiently in the therapy. How this matter is resolved may well not be clear. The supervisor may disallow attempting to work through the difficulty in supervision; a return to therapy may not be feasible.

However a third method of training therapists placed greater emphasis on trainees' supervision rather than their personal therapy. This group of trainees was mainly drawn from professions that are influenced by psychoanalytic methodology, such as counselling, social and probation work, and the training of psychiatrists. Ekstein and Wallerstein's (1972) distinctive contribution to supervision was to shift it away from concentrating solely on the trainee's professional development. While they recognised that the functions of a supervisor and therapist are different and must remain separate, they suggested that supervision could not be merely a form of didacticism, but that countertransference problems, the relationship to the supervisor and the affective problems of learning, must also be considered by the trainee's supervisor. This marked a considerable development in supervision practice and increased the skills needed by supervisors.

However, despite important advancements in understanding the task and complexity of supervision, formal supervision was still only considered as a training requirement. Post qualification, supervision had no place in a therapist's professional structure. Any use of supervision remained, as it still does, the personal choice of the individual.

The gradual emergence of supervision as a tool to be used outside and beyond training began as an organisational response to concern about the practices of Scientology and 'brainwashing' which had somehow become connected to the practice of counselling in the public's mind. In an attempt to reassure the public and to protect the profession from becoming discredited, an umbrella body, the British Association of Counselling and Psychotherapy, mandated that counsellors accredited by them must be in regular ongoing supervision for the whole of their professional life.

This encouragement to therapists to open up their practices to a supervisor was a good idea, but one that did not necessarily succeed in its intention. One obvious reason for this is that supervision requires trust, mutual respect, and a willingness to learn and to change. It is impossible for supervisors to have a detailed overview of all cases in which a therapist may be engaged. If a therapist wishes to avoid bringing certain cases or issues to supervision it is relatively easy to do. Therefore the idea that compulsory supervision in itself would protect the public from malpractice was not born out in practice. Abusive therapists could not only continue to abuse their clients without detection, they could now also abuse their supervisors (see also Chapter 9).

While supervision was increasingly used within the profession as part of good practice, confusingly the same term was also being used within the profession as one of the disciplinary measures used when dealing with errant therapists. That 'supervision' was used outside the profession in reference to disciplinary processes caused even more confusion. Rather like the word 'counselling', the word 'supervision' has been somewhat devalued by its loose definition.

The Viennese model has tended to reinforce supervision as a separate activity from therapy or analysis with a different frame of reference. While accepting that the understanding and interpretation of the transference is central to the therapeutic relationship, supervision has tended to neglect its impact with the supervisory couple, concentrating on the transference, and counter-transference activities of the supervisee and patient. The rationale for supervision concentrating only on the supervisees' professional development and not their affective inner world is that the neurotic transference between themselves and their therapists has to be preserved in as undiluted a form as possible. This has led to supervision being viewed as an adult–adult relationship, a view not supported by the majority of supervisees who only too well understand the power of the transference between them and the supervisor. Searles (1986) looked at how to harness this unrecognised dynamic while keeping intact the triadic nature of supervision. Drawing on Heimann's (1950) seminal paper on counter-transference he concluded that monitoring and interpreting the supervisee's emotional reactions to the supervisor gave important insights into the patient's unconscious.

While the notion of blank screened therapists not showing their emotions towards their patients still persists more or less as a myth, the notion that a supervisor should be blank screened still has a lot of influence on current supervision practice. Ekstein and Wallerstein's (1958) work on the training of therapists draws on Heimann's (1950) and Searle's (1986) work. In a sense the position of Ekstein and Wallerstein's trainees is analogous to the position of trained therapists in ongoing supervision. Having completed their own therapy their supervisory relationship is the only professional relationship in which their own and their patient's inner worlds are referenced. The transference between supervisor and supervisee is significant not only for the patient's well being but for the supervisee's mental health. Perhaps it is time to re-evaluate the Hungarian model of supervision and to suggest that it has much to offer supervisors working with supervisees who have completed their therapeutic training.

In psychodynamic supervision two processes occur simultaneously. One process involves the supervisor consciously supervising the actual work between supervisee and client. The other involves the supervisor engaging unconsciously with the client's unconscious material. It is this quite complex interaction which, if properly responded to, enables a furthering of unconscious communication from supervisor to supervisee, and supervisee to client, which is essentially therapeutic. In psychodynamic supervision the supervisor does not normally encounter the supervisee's patient either directly or through audio or videotapes. The patients are always absent; they are incarnated through the unconscious communications between them, their therapists and supervisors.

To engage therapeutically with a patient is an awesome task. An unhappy, vulnerable person has found the courage to begin therapy and to trust the therapist to explore with them. There are hypotheses that help guide the therapist; unlike physical illness psychic connections are invisible, there are no 'knee bones connecting to thigh bones!'. A hypothesis that a patient is, for example, 'borderline' is just a hypothesis. Unlike the surgeon who knows where the inflamed appendix is, the psychotherapist can never be sure where to look beneath the surface. What constitutes an interpretation, let alone a correct interpretation is much debated. The supervisor's task is no less awesome. The therapist's task is to enable the patient to express what he as yet does not know; the supervisors task is to monitor that process and to enable supervisees to express for the patient what as yet they do not know: what lies in their unconscious. As in therapy there are hypotheses and strategies to help guide the supervisor, but no certainties, no correct things to say, no sure reference points.

One model of supervision that has already been comprehensively documented is that it is essentially triangular and therefore Oedipal. Because of the way Oedipal residues are inherent in the task of supervision it has been labelled 'deadly equal' (Mattinson, 1981). Mattinson coined this phrase in a paper describing the difficulties encountered when supervisors were presenting their work for supervision. To label a triangle 'deadly equal' implies that the triangle is a congruent figure with the same angle at each of the three corners. It is this idea of sameness, symmetry, rather than congruence that illustrates the difficulties Mattinson describes, for symmetry implies death or deadliness (Bomford; 1999). A patient will seek a symmetrical relationship with the therapist as a defence against their fear of change. Therapists (supervisees) will similarly seek a symmetrical relationship with supervisors, both as part of the reflection process but also because of their own defences. However if either of these relationships is allowed to remain symmetrical then a lack of movement, stagnation and deadness will occur either in the therapy or the supervision.

Mattinson's 'deadly equal triangle' details difficulties experienced when supervisors presented supervision work for supervision. The puzzlement was that this group of supervisors appeared more fragile in this situation than in a casework discussion group. Mattinson deduced from observing this group that the problem lay in the Oedipal nature of supervision. However the difficulties observed by Mattinson in the supervision of supervision work seem also to bear close correlation to difficulties experienced when therapists (supervisees) present therapeutic work for supervision. I have listed them beginning with the least problematic and ending with the most problematic.

• presenting the details of the clinical assessment;
• describing the therapy session;
• stating the transference from patient to supervisee (therapist);
• stating what the patient said;
• stating the interpretative comments made by the supervisee (therapist);
• assessing the effectiveness of these comments through reflection on the patient's next statement(s).

The first two are relatively easy to present; more trust and skill is needed to bring the last four into the supervision. And it is in those interactions that the absent patient communicates. These difficulties appear to be present even when the supervisee presents a process recording of the therapy session. It would appear that the greater the intimacy between supervisee and patient, the greater the difficulty in describing it in supervision. It is in this area of the work that the defences of the patient or the supervisee attempt to make relationships symmetrical. It is the task of the supervisee to enable the patient towards a-symmetry; it is the task of the supervisor to enable the supervisee and patient towards a-symmetry. It is in understanding and interpreting the transference and skilful accessing of the counter-transference that provide the main skills required to assist this process for both therapist (supervisee) and supervisor. While supervision must remain focused as a three-person activity – supervisor, supervisee and patient – supervision has to actively work with the transference formed between the supervisor and supervisee as well. The quality of this transference becomes more complicated when supervising qualified therapists as unresolved transference issues between the supervisee's former therapist may significantly colour the transference relationship to the supervisor. Secrets that may have been kept during the supervisee's own therapy may become enacted in the supervisee's therapeutic work and subsequently reflected in the supervision work. This can distract from the therapeutic and the supervisory task. The fascination of supervision lies in finding how to help the supervisee understand (and resolve) these transferences and allow the patient to 'speak'.

Freud's early model of the psychic apparatus was presented as a triangle of ego, id and superego. These 'agencies' as Freud described them form the basis for projections onto either whole or part objects. Their inter-relationships may vary from neurotic negotiations between the agencies to all-out war with resulting chaos. The 'deadly equal' triangle of supervision therefore actually comprises three triangles formed by the psyches of patient (P), supervisee (T) and supervisor (S) represented by Figure 1.1.

Each triangle contains three triangulation points of the **Ego**, **Id**, and **Super-**ego as these aspects of the psyche are present in all three participants. The triangles T and S overlap with each other and both bear some relation to the triangle P. However, their not being totally restrained within the larger

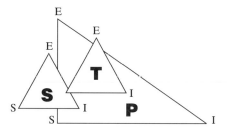

FIGURE 1.1

triangle represents the independence and greater flexibility of supervisees' and supervisors' psyches.

In a therapy session patients may well present consciously defended, and attempt symmetry either passively or aggressively with the therapist. The task of therapy is to discover the way in which the unconscious is asymmetrically challenging conscious actions. Within the patient's psyche (P) distortions will occur as the ego, superego and id engage in conflict with each other. The therapist's task is to understand how this experience communicates through the transference to allow the patient to understand and modify the distortions, enabling a metamorphosis to occur.

The distortions within the patient's psyche (P) are in turn received by the supervisee's distorted but more flexible psyche (T) thus creating the space that enables therapy to be effective. Difficulties will occur in the therapy if the distortions of the supervisee's psyche are not contained, either through insight gained by the supervisee's own therapy or through supervision, but are made the concern of the patient in the therapy session. In other words difficulties occur if the ego of the supervisee is subjected to uncontainable impulses from either the id or superego. The supervisee's psyche (T) while free floating, is restrained by the patient's defences (P). In other words if the therapy is working well the supervisee will be attempting to modify the patient's defences without dismantling them destructively. The supervisor enters into the therapeutic relationship as yet another free floating triangle (S) but one which is restrained by the patient's psychic defences (P) as well as, to a lesser extent, by the supervisee's psychic defences (T). The task of the supervisor is to relate to the distortions created by the patient/supervisee relationship (PT) to enable the supervisee and the patient to be less imprisoned (restrained, limited) by the patient's psychic defences. The ability of the supervisor to keep a free floating, hovering attitude to the work presented means that two separate (patient and therapist) and one combined (patient–therapist) distortions can be attended to. These ideas are illustrated by the following example.

A trained and experienced female supervisee, who had had extensive therapy during her training, presented work from a tertiary college to a male supervisor. She was small in stature. She presented a patient, a young woman of large stature who had asked for help with a crisis over her identity. During the presentation the supervisor was aware that he was gradually adopting a very chauvinistic stance with a preaching attitude towards the supervisee. He felt that most of her responses were wrong and that it was his job to put her to rights. With poorly focused interventions he began to do so. During the session he became uncomfortable and aware of what he was doing. He interrupted himself and invited the supervisee to reflect with him in order to understand what was happening. They discovered he was acting out the role of an absent father. In effect he was saying to the (mother) supervisee, 'I can't understand why you can't do better with this (daughter) patient. You should do what I say. Just go away and follow my instructions because I have more important things to attend to.'

In this case the patient was initially felt to be hardly contained or containable. Her psyche was a war zone and seemed to represent an unsatisfactory environment comprising debased feminine and contemptuous masculine elements. Her superego had internalised both a harsh father and a victim mother. There were no good objects in her life. Her internal conflicts were not being contained. In the therapy session the patient denigrated the supervisee into a cowed and useless mother. Instead of hearing this as a frightened child wanting firm holding the supervisee could hear only a bully. Her normally flexible ego was unable to respond to the powerful transference caused by the onslaught directed at her by the patient. Hence her seeking supervisory help. However instead of helping, the supervisor initially responded by bullying the supervisee, treating her as a weak and ineffectual partner. Had this continued the needs of the patient would not have been addressed and the supervisee, submitting to a similar experience she had had during the therapy, would not have had her needs met either. Therefore the supervisor needed urgently to make space for an internal enquiry into what was happening in the supervision.

A number of possibilities needed to be surveyed in that brief space. Was this about the supervisor's own pathology; why he was responding in such a manner? Was it about the supervisee's pathology; why she was responding to the patient as she was? Was something being enacted through the transference between the supervisor and supervisee; why they were responding to each other as they were? Because not all that was happening was necessarily the result of the reflection process.

If the supervisor had continued to react to rather than attempt to understand the chaotic internal world of the patient, the supervisor and possibly, passively, the supervisee would have been acting out some of their own distortions and their unresolved conflicts. However through understanding this as a manifestation of the patient's internal chaos the supervisory triangle could be re-established and the work of therapy and supervision could proceed.

But this stormy and difficult supervision session was indeed not all caused by the reflection process because the supervisee's difficulties reappeared over a period of a few months in two similar cases presented for supervision. When with a third patient a similar difficulty emerged the supervisor decided to initiate a discussion to consider the way in which the supervisee responded to young women of a certain size. That possibly her presenting these cases for supervision meant she was attempting to understand something about herself. Through the discussion that followed, the supervisee was enabled to rediscover an old fear of being bullied by both larger girls and her father. These events which lay back in her personal past, had been addressed in her therapy but issues remained unresolved and thus re-emerged in her work.

It is relatively easy to see pathology in patients and supervisees; it is harder for the supervisor to understand how their pathology may hinder the supervisory (and therefore the therapeutic process). Elsewhere in this book supervision of supervision is discussed – the place in which the Deadly Equal Triangle throws up its difficulties but where distortions in the supervisor's psyche can receive attention.

Was this appropriate use of supervision time? Certainly for two or three sessions the needs of her patients were ignored, all the concentration being on the supervisee's affective inner world. Should the supervisor have merely noted the difficulty and suggested the supervisee took it somewhere else? Should he have insisted according to BACP guidelines that a separate therapeutic contract be made to provide space for the supervisee to resolve this difficulty? Her difficulties could be explained by pathologising some aspect of her, or by shedding some doubts on her training therapy or training body. However any thoughts the supervisor may have which hint at either suggesting a return to further therapy or which throw doubts on the integrity of either her training therapist or training body should be treated with utmost caution. The probability is that the appropriate time for the supervisee to examine a certain defence is now, the appropriate person is this supervisor and that subjective comparison of another's training organisation is insidious and needs to be avoided.

As well as distortions appearing within the triangles of supervisee or supervisor there are other influences that can mask patients' distortions, effectively 'silencing' them before therapy has deemed to have begun. Over-zealous attention to obtaining too much information in an assessment interview, a kind of 'let's get the facts' approach, may be undesirable. Anxiety in assessment interviews that important pathology has not been missed, that the patient is indeed a suitable case for treatment can cause the patient's voice to be drowned out. The assessing therapist may unconsciously defend against something the patient has disclosed. For instance a patient's use of recreational drugs may cause the therapist to fail to hear what this means because this triggers something unresolved (maybe not appropriately confessed earlier in therapy?) by the therapist. Paradoxically in supervision, lack of gathering detail can equally mask the patient's distortion. The reluctance to ask for certain details to be clarified has been clearly in evidence from supervisors in training. As part of the course requirements in the WPF Counselling and Psychotherapy's Diploma in Supervision Course supervision trainees are asked to supervise a fellow trainee's therapeutic work while being observed by their peers and by staff members. In part because of the anxiety this exercise generates trainees frequently fail to ask for detail. Initially the supervisory pair often attempt to deal with their anxiety by telling each other, in their introductory contract, that there is symmetry in their philosophy, that they, for example, both work psychodynamically. Sometimes this does not allow them to hear the asymmetry; the way each other differs in the manner in which they approach the patient. During the presentation they fail to enquire about small details such as time keeping; dress and changes of dress; the way the fee is negotiated and how it is paid; changes in how the patient arrives and departs. So simple questions such as, 'what has changed?', 'what do you charge?', 'has there been a recent change in the way the patient has arrived or left?' can allow the supervisor sufficient detail for the patient to emerge effectively during the supervision session.

The preservation of patient confidentiality has, on occasions led to the practice of using pseudonyms when presenting work in supervision. This impairs the effectiveness of the patient's communication. Names give identity. In fantasy we have an internal picture of the person behind a name. Partly this will be a sum of the Michaels and Marys we have met, partly it will be from the collective unconscious. Thus a supervisor whose background is in the Judaic/Christian tradition will colour differently from a Muslim supervisor the Michaels, Matthews and Marys encountered. How a name is used: full, shortened, a nickname or a childish name carried over into adulthood give clues to pathology and help the patient to communicate. A 'Fred' can never be renamed 'Harry' in supervision 'to preserve confidentiality' without disturbing the unconscious connection the patient and supervisee may have with the name 'Fred'. However if a supervisee or organisation insists on pseudonyms being used then one of the supervisor's tasks is to wonder why the supervisee chose to name 'Fred', 'Harry'.

Take for example the now famous case in which Jung asked for Freud's help, the case of Sabina Spielrein, cited as the first recorded use of supervision. When Jung first presented this case he kept her identity secret. He presents her merely as a 'difficult case' and described her by her pathology. Because of this anonymity an important aspect of Spielrein's difficulties, perhaps not noticed by Jung was not conveyed to Freud. This may well have caused frustration and have been one reason why she makes herself known by writing directly to Freud ('the supervisor' as it were) requesting a consultation. In so doing Freud came to know her both as a 'difficult case' and as Sabina Speilrein. The name of the patient communicated another facet, an additional colour to the mere description of her symptoms because the name 'Spielrein' means, 'play clean'. What did this signify for Sabina and for the family for the family name forms part of her history and therefore of her story? As Jung (1972: 145) stated 'the crucial thing is the story (which) shows the human background and the human suffering and only at that point can the therapy begin to operate'. At the time at which Spielrein wrote to Freud, other parties had become involved and other letters were exchanged. One from Emma Jung (Carotenuto, 1984) to Spielrein's parents warned them of Jung's sexual interest in their daughter. They responded by requesting an interview with Jung. He replied that if he is paid as a doctor then there would be a guarantee of no sexual involvement; if however he is not paid then 'one would have to leave matters to fate'. From this comment a scandal ensued. Was Spielrein being seductive? Was she attempting to, or had she actually, seduced her therapist? Had her therapist seduced her? Was she playing dirty? Was the therapist playing dirty, by not revealing all to the supervisor, or by seducing the patient? Speilrein's father, described as a cuckolded man who would break into the all-too-magic circle of his wife and first born daughter to enjoy spanking the child for his own pleasure (Kerr, 1994), doesn't seem to be exactly a clean player either. So we have a patient carrying the family name of 'clean play' bringing into her therapy an inner little abused girl, unconsciously involved in dirty play.

In his correspondence with Freud, Jung did not 'come clean' that readily. He silenced his patient's attempts at communication through supervision by omitting to tell Freud of her desire to have a child by him and to tell him that her chosen name for this child would be Siegfried. This evidences the proposition made earlier in this chapter that describing a patient's pathology in supervision is much easier than allowing the supervisor into the intimacy of the therapeutic intercourse. Most supervisees have at some time or other suppressed detail they find embarrassing to recount or feared their supervisor would not approve of. Silencing patients' communications thwarts the urge for creativity and progress coming from them.

When Jung first wrote to Freud about Speilrein he asked if he could 'abreact'; that is to relieve himself of a complex by reliving repressed fantasies or experiences in feeling or action. It is an interesting communication because it suggests that Jung was asking for more from Freud than just help or good advice. Probably he used the word abreact because the early analysts' hypothesis was that mentioning (confessing) something was sufficient to effect psychic healing. The hypothesis of 'working through' came later.

Until a cache of her letters was discovered about 25 years ago, Speilrein was literally a footnote in psychoanalytic history. When we read Jung's work, *The Psychology of the Transference* (1954) we therefore find no direct reference to his experience with her, yet it is hard not to feel the text is imbued with the encounter he had with his first analytic patient. In this work Jung makes a number of telling comments on the power of the transference, the 'alpha and omega' of the analytic method as he called it. It has direct reference to the task of supervision even if occasionally his descriptive language may be thought to be extreme. He writes about the power of the transference, about how the overpowering contents of a patient's mind can infect and fascinate the therapist. The therapist can feel as transfixed, obsessed is Jung's word, rather like a rabbit caught in the headlights of a car cannot move to safety unless helped. As far as Jung is concerned experience counts for little when caught in a strong transference relationship, a relationship founded on mutual unconsciousness. This can be dangerous for the therapist, for to quote Jung's words 'unconscious infection brings with it the therapeutic possibility – which should not be under-estimated – of the (patient's) illness being transferred to the (therapist)' (1954: 365).

In his old age Jung again returns to themes probably influenced by his encounter with Speilrein. Reflecting on the theme of the 'wounded healer' Jung suggests that while the therapist is in danger of being infected by the patient's illness, the patient is in danger of being 'exactly the right plaster for the (therapist's) sore spot' (1972: 156). If experience does not offer protection, then, Jung suggests, all therapists should have a supervisor for the whole of their professional life. Jung calls supervisors 'confessors' perhaps influenced by his experience when a young man of needing to 'abreact' to Freud. This implies that Jung considered separating therapy and supervision into two distinct and separate activities was not helpful for either patients or therapists. Jung called supervisors 'confessors' because in his mind supervision went far further than quality control or touching up on technique or being offered a different perspective. Jung recommended confessional supervision to protect the patient from the therapist's unconscious collusion, and, as importantly, to protect the sanity of the therapist.

The Hungarian model had supervisees working with their training therapists and bringing the affect of the patient in their therapy. The necessary modification of this model demands that supervision includes as much about the patient/supervisee transference and counter-transference as it does about the supervisee/supervisor transference and counter-transference. It can hurt to acknowledge as a supervisee that one has erotic, murderous, hatred feelings or, perhaps worse still, total indifference towards a patient. To quote Jung again 'When the doctor wears his personality like a suit of armour, he has no effect' (1972: 155). If supervisees can be attacked by their patients for their apparent mistakes and weaknesses these supervisees may be working from an inner strength for therapists are only effective when affected themselves. When presenting in supervision, such revelations can feel very persecutory. The trainee supervisee may fear assessment and judgement. Trained supervisees may fear criticism of professional competence. Good supervision might be construed as an activity in which supervisors use their critical judgement to make sense of the patient material. Through reference to their counter-transference and use of their intuition they hope to understand how the patient has affected the supervisee.

Psychodynamic supervision is the space in which the absent patient communicates through the shared fantasies of supervisor and supervisee. The supervisee brings an image of the patient, created in the transference relationship with the patient. This image is modified by the supervisee's own training, therapy and life experience. This will be 'heard' by the supervisor through the transference/counter-transference relationship established in the supervision. What the patient is 'saying' will be discussed and modified through the discussion in supervision. The internal image of the patient brought to supervision is created in the minds of the supervisor and supervisee and in the space between them. Both carry the potential to be the patient, both are responsible for the patient's welfare. This implies that clinical responsibility, is essentially a shared responsibility.

If dreams are construed as the 'royal road' to the unconscious, counter-transference is the motorway rivalling dreams for speed of access. Reflection (or parallel) process is the supervisors' slip road to the unconscious of both patient and supervisee. In supervision training, trainee supervisors spend much time in discussion about the boundary between supervision and therapy. Some think that the difference should be obvious and external. Some attempt this by social engineering. A cup of coffee, or of not charging for a missed supervision session is one method adopted in an attempt to ensure the difference is marked. Placing a reliance on the fantasy that supervision is an adult–adult relationship is another. Other supervisors attempt to manage the boundary by focusing entirely on the work presented and only concern themselves with the supervisee's professional performance. However such a focus can easily be experienced as persecutory by the supervisee. All can easily suppress the communication of the silent patient who needs to be heard.

All who have been in supervision will have recognised their own regression. Regression allows things to be taken in and learning to take place. Thus the supervisor will inevitably need to take into account the distortions of the supervisee's psyche. It took nearly 40 years for the counter-transference to be recognised as a useful tool. Some 50 years after Searles wrote about the use of counter-transference and the emotional value of the supervisor's response the notion still exists that supervision can be organised separately from therapy. Perhaps the early founders of the Hungarian school of training were right to indicate that false divisions between therapy and supervision impoverish the work and that successful clinical supervision needs to have access to the affective inner worlds of all three participants.

References

Bomford, R. (1999) *The Symmetry of God*. London: Free Association Books.

Carotenuto, A. (1984) *A Secret Symmetry*. London: Routledge.

Ekstein, R. and Wallerstein, R. (1972) *The Teaching and Learning of Psychotherapy*. Madison, CT: International Universities Press, Inc.

Heimann, P. (1950) '*On counter-transference*' in M. Tonnesmann (ed.) *About Children and Children No-Longer*. London: Routledge. pp. 73.

Jung C.G. (1954) *The Psychology of the Transference* (Collected works, 16). London: Routledge.

Jung, C.G. (1972) *Memories, Dreams, Reflections*. London: Fontana Books.

Kerr, J (1994). *A Most Dangerous Method*. London: Sinclair Stevenson.

Mattinson, J. (1981) *The Deadly Equal Triangle*. Northampton, MA and London: The Smith College School of Social Work and the Group of the Advancement of Psychotherapy in Social Work.

Searles, H.F. (1986) 'The informational value of the supervisor's emotional experiences', in *Collected Papers on Schizophrenia and Related Subjects*. London: Maresfield Library.

Chapter 2

The Transition from Therapist to Supervisor

Mary Banks

Can you become enlightened and penetrate everywhere without knowledge?

Ch'u ta-Koa (1937)

The task of turning therapists into supervisors is a complex but fascinating one as so much depends on the intrinsic personality of the therapist, and, in turn, the personality of the supervisor, which must also have a major influence. These are the very reasons why my chapter must inevitably contain some exposure – not only of the therapists whose supervision I am describing, but also of myself and my own particular theoretical and philosophical stance. In my own investigation into the personality of people working in the mental health field (Banks, 1997), I found that the work tended to be attractive to those who had an impulse to heal. This tendency could arise out of multiple factors, i.e. empathy towards the wounded patients by identification; narcissistic need for omnipotence; reaction formation; use of work and patients as a transitional object; struggle to resolve Oedipal conflicts as well as other features which will be elaborated on as the chapter progresses. In addition to the important factor of the personalities of the therapist and supervisor, another major element exists in the complex network experienced in the transference and counter-transference which develops.

Just as much as it is a gift to be able to work therapeutically with patients, so it can be rewarding to enable and witness the growth and development of therapists into supervisors, by discussion and example. They will in turn become supervisors, mentoring their own group of apprentices who will come to value them. Turning what has been offered in the supervisory arena into a script that is compatible with a therapist's own personality and interests is the essence of supervision. The question of how the supervisor manages this task will be explored in this chapter.

The past of each of us comments on the present, and without the past there is no future. This is the story of the emergent supervisor, because it speaks about the development from patient to therapist to supervisor.

Each patient is the central figure in their own story and in that story each of us, whether friend, partner, relative, therapist or supervisor plays a vital but secondary role. One crucial difference between the therapist and the supervisor and the other characters in the story lies in the distance maintained by these professionals from the day to day lives of the patient: indeed, the supervisor is not consciously known about at all. The other factor is the training and analysis that the professionals have undertaken in order to foster a therapeutic relationship. Thus, the possibility of 'an island of intellectual contemplation' (Sterba, 1934: 124) is introduced by the supervisor to the therapist, and in turn to the central figure of the patient, the impact rippling outwards to the rest of the characters in the story and back again in an interactive way. The professionals do not write the script but, Sterba postulates, through interpretations made in the analytic relationship, they facilitate the patient's understanding of the part they play in their own history. The benefits and effects of this unfolding in the therapeutic relationship move the patient towards an acceptance of self. Offering this 'island' takes skill evolved from years of training and personal analysis or therapy, as well as a myriad of contemplative states such as empathy, intuition, curiosity and self-knowledge, which is central to the therapist's ability to 'penetrate everywhere'. This basic stance is enhanced by the more formal external factor of learnt theory, which then allows the possibility of supporting or questioning therapeutic formulations.

As psychotherapists we work with the scenes presented to us. We try to discover the script that is being uncovered, to follow the story as it emerges by immersing ourselves in it and observing our reaction to it. We attempt to use the counter-transference as a servant rather than a master (Segal, 1981), employing the tools of detection and ultimately interpretation. Each of us offers a unique response to our patients, and by extension our supervisees, *born of our own psychopathology* and experiences (Banks, 1997). We all use our 'selves' as the principal tool to work with the people who consult us.

The giving of ourselves is complicated and can be likened to a doctor prescribing medication. Freud suggested that 'It is not a modern dictum but an old saying of physicians that these diseases are not cured by the drug but by the physician, that is, the personality of the physician in as much as through it he exerts a mental influence' (1905: 259). This is a view that Balint (1957) endorsed: 'the most frequently used drug in general practice was the doctor himself, i.e. that it was not only the bottle of medicine or the box of pills that mattered, but the way the doctor gave them to his patient – in fact, the whole atmosphere in which the drug was given and taken' (1957: 1). It is the individuality of each psychotherapist which determines how they give of themselves and in what dosage. Behind the training is the person, the raw material, the essence of what we are and can or cannot give. In the giving of ourselves we use the experience of merging and separating to understand and distinguish the unique characteristics of the other person. Some pieces of the story presented by the patient may be missing, but more crucially they may be missed by the listener if empathy, for example, is absent. As in all drama, identification with the characters enables the viewer to engage with the plot, to become a part of it, while maintaining a distance. To put this another way, it is those who know about suffering who have the ability to immerse themselves in the suffering of others.

Stein (1984) nicely describes Jung's notion of the therapeutic task: 'administering the medicine occurs by way of the counter-transference/transference process . . . recommending some healing ritual, or even making acutely empathic interpretations' (1984: 78). He compares current analytic concepts of mutual identification, projective identification and introjection to aspects of the shamanic cycle. This comparison provided me with a useful metaphor when I undertook a research project (Banks, 1997) on the unconscious factors in the personality of the mental health worker. By immersing myself in the 'shared world' of all healers, I came to a deeper understanding of the processes and problems of the psychoanalytic psychotherapist and, as I shall show, of the factors that can help or impede the therapist's development as a supervisor.

The healers I studied were motivated by their history – just as it seems likely that our shamanic ancestors were motivated by theirs. Those of us who work in an analytic framework have, as part of our training and personal development, entered into psychoanalysis or psychotherapy as patients in an attempt to master our conflicts. Freud (1900) himself offered an excellent role model by subjecting himself to intense scrutiny, which he then described in *The Interpretation of Dreams*. However, he was aware of an element of danger in overcoming distress: 'no one who, like me, conjures up the most evil of those half formed demons that inhabit the human breast and seek to wrestle with them, can expect to come through unscathed' (Freud 1901: 109).

The shared world of the healers

In some parts of the world, such as native North America, the Shamans are believed to be the original healers. Although today there is a growing body of scientific knowledge about the causes of human unhappiness, the Shaman can be seen to have a modern-day counterpart in today's psychotherapeutic healers.

Ninian Smart (1969) gives an interesting account of the Shamans. In tribal societies they occupied a special professional position alongside priests and medicine men, and were thought to have a 'gift for ecstasy' and to be able to mediate with the spirit world. After a long, rigorous training involving self-discipline and meditation, the Shaman emerged transformed and 'imbued with authority to speak of the spirit-world, from which they have, as it were, returned' (1969: 59). Anthropological studies (Eliade, 1964; Lommel, 1967) of these cultures reveal that the prospective Shaman is able to cure others by undergoing and overcoming intense distress and illness, and that 'he was or is a sick man, a man in every way underprivileged, a man who began his life with a false start' (Lommel, 1967: 32). Lommel goes on to say that, if the prospective Shaman did not ascend to psychic rebirth through overcoming this mental sickness, the result was insanity or death.

Traditionally the holy men in India similarly gain their power and authority from inner experience, in their case born out of such austere practices as sitting in the midday sun surrounded by burning fires, the 'heat of self repression' leading to a '. . . sense of vision or release and this meant a new knowledge. Knowledge is power' (Smart, 1977: 41). In this activity the mystics go into a trance and merge with the fire.

Each type of mystic will give his quest a distinctive flavour, but despite external and mental differences it is possible to believe that they all experience a similar inner light. In the *Tao Tê Ching* by Ch'u ta-Kao (1937: 45), written by the philosopher Lao Tzu (meaning 'old master') during or some time after Confucius's day, this type of experience, which epitomises the heart of self-discovery and the consequent understanding of others, is encapsulated:

> He who knows other is wise;
> He who knows himself is enlightened.
> He who conquers others is strong;
> He who conquers himself is mighty.
> He who knows contentment is rich.
> He who keeps on his course with energy has will.
> He who does not deviate from his proper place will long endure.

An interpretation of this was made by Han Fei-tsu in the *Tao Tê Ching*: 'The difficulty of knowing does not lie upon seeing others, but upon seeing oneself. Therefore he who sees himself is enlightened' (Ch'u ta-Kao 1937: 45).

Within both the nature of the mystic and the society in which they play an accepted part there is a reverence for what psychotherapists have come to call the unconscious. There is an expectation that the mystic and his followers will submit themselves unquestioningly to a process. In turn, utterances from the mystic are not subject to unfolding exploration.

Jung (1946) explicitly adopted the shamanic model of healing, in that he believed that the therapist needs to be vulnerable to (in other words, to merge with) patients' illnesses. He described this as catching an 'unconscious infection', which activates the therapist's own latent conflicts. The suffering by the analyst propels him or her towards identification of the cause of the patient's pain.

The old healers were given authority by society – by those who looked up to them and respected their place in the culture they shared with them. The question for us is how budding supervisors can find their own authority as teachers in a society which does not always have a respected place for its healers, let alone accept their utterances unquestioningly.

Thinking for one's self in a free space

Supervision is inevitably an intrusion into the therapeutic dyad, where it may be welcomed or resented. From the patient's point of view, though consciously unaware of the supervisor, the wish to own the therapist exclusively echoes a wish to remain in the pre-Oedipal phase. Therapists who collude with this and resent supervision as an intrusion may find it difficult to think about or stand up to the patient in their care. Furthermore, for those working to a bio-medical model, such as doctors, whose discipline involves working towards professional autonomy through a hierarchical structure, supervision can appear to diminish the status of the therapist, who seems to remain for ever a disciple. However, for the therapist, the notion of valuing the other, rather than bowing to authority, lies at the heart of modern day practice. Thus the hierarchical pyramid of supervision can gradually change to that of a matrix made up of many possibilities allowing a work discussion between peers, each of whom has something precious to contribute. The experience of identifying, adapting and consolidating the perceived external, as a complement to one's own personality, gives rise to the idea of a meeting of equals. The task for supervisees, then, is to play their part in the supervision relationship by speaking honestly about their work and receiving the thoughts of the supervisor, rather than projecting omniscient powers onto the supervisor, which can lead to learning by imitation and rote.

Where the Shamans had a philosophy from which they took their lead, psychoanalysis provides a theory of the personality, with its inner psychic reality and shared external reality, and a theory of psychoanalytic technique. This is the 'knowledge' of psychoanalysis – developed through individual exploration yet built upon the foundation provided by previous analysts. What psychoanalysis does not provide is a philosophy in which its practitioners have to believe. In 1949 one such analyst, Paula Heimann described a most important concept for those of us wanting to play a part on the analytic stage today. 'The analyst's emotional response to his patient within the analytic situation represents one of the most important tools for his work. The analyst's counter-transference is an instrument of research into the patient's unconscious' (1989: 74).

Thus, within the boundaries of training, supervision takes place in a free space like therapy or analysis. The trainee has a choice within their organisation's list of approved practitioners. Selecting a supervisor partly sets the scene for the development of the trainee's future professional identity. Supervisors of modern day psychotherapists consider discovery and creation, which arc truc to the practitioner, an essential factor in one's own original psychoanalytic cultural blueprint.

In the shared world of the healers then, certain concepts link the old to the new. These include rigorous training; the authority that the shaman and the psychotherapist is given by those they are attempting to heal; and a sense of vocation, in that both go into this work because of certain needs which have been unfulfilled. Both have the ability to identify with, but also stand back from, the patient.

What is different is that contemporary psychoanalytic psychotherapists work to disinvest themselves of the authority and omniscience projected onto them by their patients. We have to work thinking that we do not always know.

Yet somehow the ideal of a therapist can be encapsulated in Lao Tzu's sayings: wisdom, enlightenment, strength, might, will, endurance and richness are woven into the words of 'knowing' and 'conquering'.

In reflecting upon the healer personality I find links between Lao Tzu's words and contemporary practice in the play between polar opposites – omnipotence/powerlessness; masochism/sadism; intimacy/distance; masculine/feminine. To draw on Chinese philosophy the complementary principle hypothesises that two forms of knowledge together provide a dynamic tension similar to the Yin-Yang polarity. In the concept of polarity, life itself exists. We, as psychotherapists, search for integration, or a space between these polar opposites in which human agency, or subjectivity, or even creativity can be found.

The impulse to heal and the personality of the healer

Bion's (1990) concept of the 'container' mother who uses reverie to contain and respond to her baby's communication, and Winnicott's (1965) concept of the mother who 'holds' at the very beginning her infant's ego, which is assumed to be only potential at the start of life, are two models for psychotherapists who listen and try to understand their patients' communications. These abilities are both satisfying to those who practise them, but they can also be a source of stress. Each of us may identify particular difficulties that can cause disharmony within our 'self' such as containing our own feelings and responses to mechanisms of projection, the development of negative, or even positive, transference and counter-transference. The question Konrad (1975) asks in his book about a psychiatric social worker's view of his clients is: 'why should I of all people be saddled with these outcasts?'

Perhaps all of us who have the impulse to heal are drawn towards suffering. Do we indeed minister to the suffering 'outcast' parts of ourselves by projectively identifying with others and recognising the outcast in them? In doing so, do we too perhaps make ourselves into outcasts? Between the giver (healer) and taker (patient) there is a special partnership that does not rest on the altruistic concept of 'giving' alone, but also on the psychological gratification of the mutuality of 'receiving'. It seems that therapists can mature and benefit from working with their clients, as well as choosing an orientation and method of practice that reduces their own psychic tensions. Schafer encapsulates the negative aspects of this as follows:

> One way or another, the analyst's temptation is to use the analytic work to get otherwise unavailable gratification, support faltering defences, enhance grandiose fantasies, and in the end, to *use* the analysand rather than to *work for* him or her.
>
> How much the analysand's sense of danger within the analysis depends on the frequency and extent of the analyst's nonneutral violations in this respect! (1983: 25)

Freud (1930) believed that, given free choice, we all pick our area of work precisely because it represents the sublimated expression of fixated drives.

Clearly, if this is so, then the task we have chosen, as wounded healers, of healing others is nigh impossible unless we are highly aware of our selves. It takes skill and self-understanding in the therapist to use sublimation positively, for the patient's benefit as well as for their own.

In my work as a therapist and as a supervisor to other healers, I have been struck by a constellation of personality traits in therapists which seem to be quite pervasive; chief among them are a narcissistic need for omnipotence and a struggle to resolve the Oedipal conflict. Others include an attempt to repair the damaged mother; empathy towards the wounded patients by identification; reaction formation; the attempt to master personal conflicts; the use of work and patients as a transitional object; and the dyads of sado-masochism, rescue and reparation, and power and control. In the following I endeavour to explore some of these features systematically, in order to give shape to the healer personality.

Narcissistic need for omnipotence

Fenichel confirms the idea that 'analysts might make impersonal use of the relationship to the patient for some unconscious purpose, such as soothing over of anxiety, satisfaction of narcissistic needs, easing of intrapsychic conflicts' (1982: 27). In other words, patients can be used (or some might say, abused) as mirroring or idealised self objects (Kohut, 1971), by therapists searching for *narcissistic omnipotence*. The therapist seeks, and indeed is wedded to, a mirroring self object that provides empathic and admiring responses to confirm a sense of self.

While much creative work in mental health lies in empathy towards wounded patients by *identification*, this can also be problematic. Kohut (1971) sets his model of narcissistic disturbance around a concept of a 'self' which is assumed to have reached coherence when the baby reaches individuation/separation from the mother as a toddler. Winnicott (1965) builds his model of human psychological development on the idea of the 'self' emerging from the infant/mother merger within a facilitating environment during infancy, in which the mother 'mirrors' for the infant the essence of their subjective experience. When the mirroring between self (patient) and object (therapist) in the therapeutic relationship breaks down, the result can be at worst a regression into pathology; alternatively, the patient may simply stop attending.

Mrs S. was a supervisee in her forties, with considerable difficulties in addressing the negative transference in her patients. In consequence the work was cosy but often unsatisfactory and greatly lacking in substance. In the supervision sessions she often had a curious, watchful expression on her face, as if she was waiting with enormous anticipation for positive strokes from me, which I found quite disconcerting. It was as if she wanted me to adore her and fuel her narcissism. We had to look into her own psychological difficulties more thoroughly than would be usual in a supervisory relationship. This is because we found that her patients would move only so far, then terminate. She experienced this as a narcissistic wounding.

It appeared to occur owing to a failure to explore the negative transference, which itself the therapist disliked as an invasion of the cosy. It seemed likely that the expectation of, and wish for, 'mirroring' approval that she did not receive from her mother was repeating itself in all relationships. Perhaps as a result of our work together she returned to therapy.

Something that I have become acutely aware of through working with narcissistic individuals is confirmed by Kernberg who suggests that people with a narcissistic character display 'a remarkable absence of interest in and empathy for others in spite of the fact that they are so eager to obtain admiration and approval from other people' (1967: 635). Their identification with the ego ideal and ideal object are so inflated that they only know themselves. He also proposes that they are empty and confused about their identity.

In this example my supervisee, Mrs A., who was in her thirties, grasped any concept on clinical technique in a wholesome and creative way and indeed executed her therapeutic duty to the letter of the psychoanalytic law, as if wanting my unreserved approval and by extension her patients' approval. However, as time went by I realised that she did not have feelings for her patients – whether revulsion, love or indeed any sort of empathic response. It seemed that there was no sense of difference. I found this disturbing, for it left me feeling empty and cold, a reflection, I would guess, of her internal world. I used my sense of shock at my supervisee's response to her patients to demonstrate my concern that such an essential tool, the counter-transference, was absent. She did become a supervisor but eventually found her niche in the academic world, which she appeared to use as a static, predictable text that did not grow or change between encounters. Indeed, she saw only what interested her. It seemed that she was retreating to a two person relationship (i.e. her relationship with the text), in order to strengthen the narcissistic mirror and avoid the hazards of the three cornered Oedipal situation.

Both therapists treated their patients as idealised self objects. In the first example, I as the supervisor was also treated in this way. Searles (1965) called this the 'Pygmalion complex': the therapist is gratified by the patient's development as a result of the care given, as if the patient is a narcissistic extension of the therapist. Thus, the patient is the mirror. Hammer (1972) and Lampl-de-Groot (1954) regard overevaluation of the self in the therapist as a defence against inferiority, a compensation for being narcissistically wounded. The narcissistic therapist will tend to cultivate the positive transference in order to ensure continued adoration from their patients. The omnipotent position they cherish owes much to the idealisation and reverence to which they are often subjected by their patients – as if they were indeed Shamans and holymen. This is dangerous ground for the supervisor too, for while it is normal to be gratified by genuine improvement and healthy to accept one's part in it, it can foster a stifling of independent thought in the supervisee and this may be invisible to an overgratified supervisor. False-self personalities are good at making patients and supervisees feel good about themselves but they may not then notice the lack of vitality in the work.

In their need to be mirrored, those with a narcissistic pathology adapt endlessly to the patient's or supervisee's demands. Insights inevitably cause the supervisee painful feelings. The supervisor's task is not to hold back from commenting on the supervisee's presentation of the work, but to be encouraging and empathetic enough not to let them leave suffering a further narcissistic wound. In contrast, students with a well developed self can bear to know that they are not omnipotent and can learn from mistakes.

The conflict

In contrast to the narcissistic dyad, the Oedipus complex tells the story of the intrapsychic experience of triangular relationships and the conflicts involved in choosing and navigating one or other point of the interpersonal triangle. It is a developmental stage that, if unresolved, may have consequences for those choosing to work in the world of healing.

In the earlier examples, neither therapist had, it seemed, resolved their identifications in a satisfactory way. Mrs S. is still working as a therapist. She struggles hard to reach her inner authority through supervision and continuing her analysis. The other therapist was not capable of integrating a concept of difference, including gender difference, into her psyche and in consequence withdrew from this field of work.

The process of socialisation encourages behaviour that is appropriate for the gender stereotype of that culture. Our society still tends to expect women to be emotionally open and nurturing and men to be emotionally inhibited, assertive and interpersonally distant, although this perception is gradually changing. Therapists are usually seen as people who have developed the so-called feminine aspects of their character; as Eisendorfer states, 'the aggressive masculine tendency "to be doing" must be subordinated to this passive capacity to listen and understand' (1959: 375). However, it might also be considered that the person is more whole if they have access to both their 'masculine' and 'feminine' traits or, to put it another way, the space between the yin and the yang.

In my research into the healer personality, I found a tendency for the healer to be more closely identified with a supportive mother than with a challenging father, stemming from unresolved conflicts of the Oedipal period. As much as it could be viewed as disadvantageous to be Oedipally fixated, however, it could also be seen as producing certain advantages, provided the healer can slowly overcome the more limiting problems stemming from the Oedipal phase of development.

Those with access to the maternal attitude considered normal for women in our society are well suited to the occupation of therapist. Equally, 'authority', which may be required in the therapeutic relationship, is stereotypically viewed as a male attribute. Used wisely both attributes can be positive traits in therapists and the accommodation of both positions in one person could be seen as a powerful medium in work with patients. Oedipally fixated women and men may need to use the role of therapist to integrate their conflicting gender identifications, working out the dimension of authority that is called for in healing work alongside the empathetic dimension.

Freud considered the core complex of the male patient to be the masculine protest against the father. The male supervisee who has difficulties in the transference he develops towards his female supervisor may be relating to her as the father who has to be rebelled against. Splitting can also evolve in the Oedipal situation. For example, the supervisor can become the feeding mother, in which case the supervisee might regard his analyst or another supervisor as a father who should get out of the way when the child has passionate desires for the mother.

Authority is very dependent on the extent to which we, as supervisors, deal with the unconscious and unavoidable transference relationship that develops in supervision. However, authority is not just in our own hands: obviously the supervisee too has to deal with the underlying transference in the relationship with the patient. Supervisors are not made of stone, so when a supervisee challenges our authority, it can cause anxiety. However awareness of such anxieties helps overcome them. We supervisors should have enough of a providing mother within us to be nurturing, but also enough of a potent father to set limits.

An example comes to mind of a male supervisee who tested my authority to the limit by his continuous need to compete with me. Whatever I offered he had already thought of, or he introduced another way of working which was at odds with the analytic. He desperately needed my help, but for a long time it was almost impossible for him to acknowledge my contribution. He even made a point of letting me know, in a particularly rivalrous manner, that he charged more than me, when I put up his fees on one occasion! My impulse with this therapist was to react to my anger and anxiety about his seeming attack on me and the working style, by getting drawn into exercising a more authoritarian stance than with which I would normally feel comfortable.

This example illustrates an Oedipal situation in which both rebellion and challenge to my authority were present. In the transference I became the authority figure of father, as was the supervisee to his patients. Through understanding these dynamics, I was able to contain the overwhelming anxiety displayed by him and moderate my authoritarian impulses towards him, thus freeing and balancing the nurturing with the potent. In consequence the quality of the therapist's relationships to his patients improved, for our relationship had allowed the possibility of both maternal and paternal identification.

Other tendencies in the healer

As I have already said, there are several other tendencies in the healer. Returning to the metaphor of the play, they could be seen as 'extras'. However, without this 'extra' support, the rest of the cast would be colourless. Thus, I will present a brief exposition of a few features that add to an understanding of the healer personality.

One of the principal ingredients of our work is *curiosity*. Without it there would be no play, for it is essential in the understanding of another and of ourselves. Curiosity leads to a conflict over *intimacy*. Often psychotherapists are attracted to their profession because of this tension between a wish for and a fear of intimacy. In my example of Mrs S., I would say that she monitored closely the intimacy she longed for in every relationship, while Mrs A. could not tolerate it at any price.

Mrs S. appeared to placate those coming into contact with her, who acted as her 'mirror'. Does this then constitute a kind of martyrdom, or *masochism*, a breeding ground for disguised *sadism*, or is it rationalised as an attitude of tolerance? There seems to be a masochistic element in wishing to relate to people who are ill and, as I stated earlier, the Shamans put themselves in danger by doing this. The 'psychic infection' that Jung (1946) describes could activate therapists' own latent conflicts and work either in their favour or against them, depending on the severity of the attack and the effectiveness of their psychic immune system. I could say, on the other hand, that Mrs A. masochistically subverted her therapeutic work, perhaps as a result of her Oedipal guilt about attacking the mother.

In the masochistic role there lies a *rescuer*. Jones (1951), talking about male therapists, puts forward the theory that the wish to 'save mother' evolves from the Oedipal situation and is a strong motive in the choice of profession of therapist. Healing the sick appears to attract people with strong *reparative* needs, indicating that there could be a lack of personal integration in the person's life which leads them to seek such a career in order to repair or rescue their patients. Rescue and reparation are closely connected, and indeed Greenson (1966) allies the two when he warns that the clinician's unconscious desire to make reparation can lead to a compulsion to rescue and behave masochistically within any object relationship. It is of interest that the rescuing fantasy has a connection particularly to unresolved narcissistic needs.

The final tendency I wish to highlight is the issue of *power*, which I see as a compensation for narcissistic wounds. The power struggle inevitably enters into human interaction in the consulting room, for the wish for power can be at the root of a desire to be a therapist. Listening to and understanding another evolves from reflection which grows out of the to and fro of spontaneous dialogue. Conversely, Freud's (1905) analogy of the analyst as sculptor, with the patient as the 'raw material', explicitly invokes the idea of a power motive. As I have already said, when speaking of the holymen of India, 'knowledge is power' and this can apply too to the modern day psychotherapist. Indeed, in Mrs A.'s situation my view was that her inability to be empathetic towards her patients and supervisees was also connected to her need for power, which in turn distorted both her treatment of patients and her supervision work. Early omnipotent fantasies, deriving out of powerlessness and vulnerability, may play a central part in someone gravitating towards a career perceived as powerful, and controlling of others. Power is a topic that has woven its way throughout all the themes and can be linked back to the *modus operandi* of our ancestral healers, who it is said also produced magical transformations.

All the features that I have described are present to some degree in all of us and it is essential that we become aware enough of them to get them to work for us, rather than against us. It is paradoxical that Mrs S., who is not a supervisor, has more potential for such work than Mrs A., and that the former returned to analysis, while the latter attended for the bare minimum of treatment! As we have seen, the principal tool that therapists use is themselves, and this is allied to a sense of personal worth, which introduces a highly unpredictable factor even though both women in the examples had a long and rigorous training.

Transformations ...

I have used the metaphor of the play, but maybe the idea of playing itself offers a key which links the magical transformations by which Shamans and Gurus conceptualise their healing power with the modern psychoanalytic psychotherapist's understanding of patient/therapist communications as occurring in the potential space (Winnicott, 1971) between them. In this space, transitional phenomena can occur, as therapist and patient listen to each other, identify and understand the communications of the other, but also add to them their personal understanding and meaning. One way of looking at this may be that the patient and therapist, or therapist and supervisor, relate by putting 'me' aspects to the 'not me' aspects of the other's communication. As Marion Milner in 1957 (quoted in Winnicott, 1971) says, it is the creative aspect of the child's playing to see the familiar in the unfamiliar, which is the child's creation of the world but also the adult's way of meaningful communicating:

> Moments when the original poet in each of us created the outside world for us, by finding the familiar in the unfamiliar, are perhaps forgotten by most people; or else they are guarded in some secret place of memory because they were too much like visitations of the gods to be mixed with everyday thinking. (1971: 39)

When we visit the theatre where the play or playing takes place, we find a playground full of magic. Fantasy is mixed with reality, and we put our own significance onto what is communicated to us by the players. According to Winnicott (1971) magic originates in the confidence the child places in the mother. This confidence, or engagement is extended, given suitable encouragement, to all the arenas in which we play.

... and beginnings of the journey but, 'the object of the dance is not to finish: the object of the dance is to dance' (Mahoney, 1989: 32)

Supervision is a third-hand encounter. The script given to the supervisor has been edited by the patient and then the therapist, and the art of supervision is to take into account what may have been edited out. The supervisor is another voice for the patient. Supervision can be said to be about hearing, and speaking: what may not have been said or heard. As the supervisor listens, an unconscious communication from the patient can sometimes be heard in, for example, the tone of the supervisee's voice. It is like an enactment of the patient in the presence of the supervisor, almost as if there is a bit of the patient in the room. The supervisor can then act as the patient's advocate, modelling empathy and identification for the therapist.

It can be irritating to have to work by proxy and to see things only through a hazy glass. Supervision sometimes reminds me of letters sent home by Prisoners of War, with anything revealing knowledge of the enemy deleted. The smokescreen has to be penetrated in a benign way, and in doing so I come back to the idea of playing. There is, conversely, more to play with (and contend with!) in supervision than in therapy, for there is also the dimension of the transference to the supervisor from the therapist. Allowing the space afforded by the distance of supervision to be creative, rather than destructive of the supervisee's potential, depends on the supervisor's ability to take responsibility and accept maturity. It is akin to thinking of oneself as an elder in the tribe and allowing others to experience freedom, something that can only happen if you are secure in yourself and your own authority. After all, it is always easier to be critical of a script than to produce an original! While in some, becoming a supervisor is a natural progression – a rite of passage and not a pathology – not everyone has the skills to be a supervisor, or, indeed, a therapist, as my earlier examples demonstrated.

The supervisor's part could be likened to a grandparental role, in that it examines the parent/child relationship, while identifying and empathising with both. The essence of a good grandparent lies in the ability to engage with both people, while at the same time being able to stand back. In being less directly engaged, there can be a potential for greater reflectiveness, while drawing on the recources of one's own experience.

However, just as the grandparent is not the parent, so the supervisor is not the therapist, and a certain abstinence has to be observed. The supervisor, for example, does not have the right to intervene directly in the therapist's psychopathology, but can hope instead that the therapist will take something in of the supervisor's way of being, while developing their own style.

Some of the transformative moments in my own development as a supervisor took place during my psychotherapy training. These revolved around the very different style my two supervisors practised. The female supervisor had a vigorous style linking patient material to relevant concepts. The male supervisor showed a caring attitude towards me, enabling me to feel supported in my work. The transformation in me, of which I was often painfully aware, occurred in bringing both their styles together so that I could form something creative and new. This became a positive transformation, but I also found that having two supervisors who held such different styles could be problematic, leading me as the supervisee to identify strongly with one or the other. Here, then, the 'me' aspects could have given way to mimicry and imitation, or splitting and rebellion. Only through the gradual development of my internal supervisor (Casement, 1988), could I hold and use the essence of myself that I discovered in my own 'island of contemplation' to effect change in my work as a therapist.

As a therapist I encourage my patients to develop their own understanding; as a supervisor, I have to support individual supervisees in developing their skills and personalities. All of us have our own unique potential to develop, but just as it is a long road from patient to fully fledged therapist, so it is an even longer journey to make the transformation from therapist to supervisor. Thus, development and transformation can grow out of our own authenticity through processes such as intuitive enlightenment, and aligning logic to non-logical thought. This is the way of the Tao, and is my preferred philosophy. Ch'u ta-Kao puts forward the view that 'The further one travels. The less one knows' (1937: 60). So too is it with learning. In other words the object of the dance is to go on seeking knowledge, or in Winnicottian terms, to discover the world through play.

References

Balint, M. (1957) *The Doctor and His Patient and the Illness*. London: Pitman Publishing.

Banks, M. (1997) 'Unconscious factors in the personality of the healer: an exploration through the psychotherapeutic encounter'. Unpublished MA thesis, University of Hertfordshire.

Bion, W. (1990) 'Attacks on Linking', in *Second Thoughts, Selected Papers on Psychoanalysis*. London: Maresfield Library, pp. 93–109.

Casement, P. (1988) *On Learning from the Patient*. London: Routledge.

Ch'u ta-Kao (1937) *A New Translation of the Tao Tê Ching*. London: Lund Humphries.

Eisendorfer, A. (1959) 'The selection of candidates applying for psychoanalytic training', *Psychoanalytic Quarterly* 28: 374–378.

Eliade, M. (1964) *Shamanism, Archaic Techniques of Ecstasy*. New York: Bollingen.

Fenichel, O. (1982) *The Psychoanalytic Theory of Neuroses*. London: Routledge and Kegan Paul.

Freud, S. (1900) *The Interpretation of Dreams*, Standard Edition 4/5. London: The Hogarth Press.

Freud, S. (1901) *The Psychopathology of Everyday Life*, Standard Edition 6. London: The Hogarth Press.

Freud, S. (1905) *On Psychotherapy*, Standard Edition 7. London: The Hogarth Press. pp. 257–268.

Freud, S. (1930) *On Civilisation and its Discontents*, Standard Edition 21. London: The Hogarth Press.

Greenson, R. (1966) 'That "impossible" profession', *Journal of the American Psychoanalytic Association* 14(1): 9–27.

Hammer, M. (1972) *The Theory and Practice of Psychotherapy with Specific Disorders*. Springfield, IL: Charles C Thomas.

Heimann, P. (1989) 'About children and children-no-longer', in M. Tonnessmann (ed.), *Collected Papers of Paula Heimann 1942–1980* London: Tavistock/Routledge. pp. 191–205.

Jones, E. (1913/1951) 'The God complex' in E. Jones (ed.), *Essays in Applied Psychoanalysis 2*. London: Hogarth Press. pp. 244–265.

Jung, C.G. (1946/1966) *The Psychology of the Transference*, Collected Works 16. New York: Princeton University Press.

Kernberg, O. (1967) 'Borderline personality organisation', *Journal of the American Psychoanalytic Association* 15(3): 641–685.

Kohut, H. (1971) *The Analysis of the Self*. New York: International University Press.

Konrad, G. (1975) *The Case Worker*. London: Huchinson & Co.

Lampl-de-Groot, J. (1954) 'Problems of Psycho-analytic training', *International Journal of Psycho-Analysis* 35(2): 184–187.

Lommel, A. (1967) *Shamanism: The Beginnings of Art*. New York: Mc Graw-Hill.

Mahoney, M. (1989) 'The Object of the Dance' in W. Dryden and L. Spurling (eds), *On Becoming a Psychotherapist*. London and New York: Routledge. pp. 17–32.

Schafer, R. (1983) *The Analytic Attitude*. New York: Basic Books.

Searles, H. (1965) *Collected Papers on Schizophrenia*. New York: International University Press.

Segal, H. (1981) *The Work of Hanna Segal*. New York: Jason Aronson.

Smart, N. (1969) *The Religious Experience of Mankind* New York: Scribner & Sons.

Smart, N. (1977) *Background to the Long Search*. London: BBC.

Stein, M. (1984) 'Power, Shamanism, and Maieutics in the counter-transference', in N. Schwartz-Salant (ed.). Wilmette, IL: Chiron. pp. 67–87.

Sterba, R. (1934) 'The fate of the ego in analytic therapy', *International Journal of Psycho-Analysis* 15(2): 117–26.

Winnicott, D. (1965) *The Maturational Process and the Facilitating Environment*. London: Hogarth Press.

Winnicott, D. (1971) *Playing and Reality*. London: Tavistock Publications.

Chapter 3

Supervision: Between Control and Collusion

Gertrud Mander

To start with a definition: a supervisor is a psychotherapist who has assumed, by virtue of training and/or experience, the role of facilitating, observing and monitoring the therapeutic work of another psychotherapist who may be in training, in private practice or in an organisation and who requires supervision for professional support or as a condition of employment. He or she will be doing this work in the belief that every practitioner of psychotherapy (not only trainees, as is still customary in some of the profession) will at times or most of the time during their working lives be in need of another professional with whom to share and explore the problems and dilemmas they come up against in the course of their complex work and the diversity of feelings, thoughts, and practical decision making it creates for them.

Supervision has been defined as 'thinking about thinking', and this can mean a multitude of different and difficult situations arising in the therapeutic dialogue and demanding analysis, understanding and elucidation. It is a process of conceptualising and consulting with another mind. It can mean asking for validation of a working hypothesis, for a second opinion when something is not yet fully understood or for confirmation of what is only dimly perceived and requires further assisted reflection. It can, however, also lead to disagreements, cause professional complications and create ethical dilemmas of great complexity in which the supervisory task becomes threatened by undercurrents of unconscious conflict and unconscious processes characteristic of an activity that involves three (or more) persons.

Here is an example of this complexity that encapsulates many features peculiar to this meta-therapeutic activity of assisting a fellow-therapist in the conscientious pursuit of their practice.

A supervisor had not been happy with the work of a supervisee whom she supervised in a staff group of a counselling service. She had been told by the administrator that her supervisee had finished prematurely with ten out of 20 cases after only a few sessions and that this was causing concern for the clients as well as for the reputation of the service. There had also been a formal complaint by a client about the abrupt manner in which this supervisee finished a session when she requested that they stopped meeting and it seemed quite clear that this therapist found it difficult to manage firm professional boundaries and to handle negative feelings.

The supervisor felt that something decisive had to be done to alert the supervisee that there was severe dissatisfaction with the quality of her work and that she might have to improve, either by undertaking some further training or by going back into therapy to examine what had caused her to become lax and impatient. Who should deliver the warning and how could the recommendations be enforced? Was this the task of the supervisor or of the administrator and how could they cooperate to help the supervisee face herself critically and constructively in order to learn from this experience that she needed to improve the quality of her work?

This tension arises not infrequently in supervision when the supervisor becomes alerted to something the supervisee does to or with a client that could harm or damage them, deliberately or out of ignorance, for the sake of self-gratification, or to have power over them. Freud warned that if we can do good it follows that we can also do harm. The attentive supervisor does well to heed this warning, both in relation to observing the supervisee and in relation to watching herself when she interacts with the supervisee and makes supervisory interventions concerning the client. It is easy to fall into one or the other of two extremes – control or collusion – in the course of facilitating and commenting on the clinical material presented by the supervisee who is eager to receive help with her therapeutic endeavour, while fearing disapproval which might diminish her self-esteem.

The competent supervisor's steady analytic attitude, which involves attentive listening, persistent vigilance and well-dosaged supervisory interpretation of the material, aims to strike a balance so that her hypothesising and her suggesting of different theoretical perspectives or technical strategies can be experienced as offerings rather than certainties, to be taken or left in a spirit of mutuality. To control or to collude are easy options of too much or too little wielding of the authority which is invested in the supervisor as a result of the one-up, one-down relationship (Rioch, 1980) in which one person is set up to observe, assess and foster the professional work of another with a vulnerable client for whose welfare she is accountable. Both attitudes involve two-person relating, and thus ignore the presence of the third, either the supervisee, when controlling, or the client, when colluding and abdicating responsibility.

It has been remarked (Mattinson, 1975) that the Oedipal three-person nature of supervision encourages rivalry and competition in the supervisory relationship which means that control and collusion in the supervisor are related – the latter being a defence against the former and a bending over to be supportive, when challenging might be experienced as uncomfortably competitive or authoritarian.

When the mutual exploration of clinical material turns into clever didactic hypothesising on the supervisor's part she ought to be aware of the temptation to demolish the supervisee's tentative and clumsy therapeutic effort. One gets easily drawn into wielding parental power and behaving like an expert by the supervisees' expectations as much as by one's own vanity and by the desire to show off knowledge, experience and intellectual prowess.

My first experience of being supervised was fortunately a good one, in fact, it was a veritable revelation of the best example of teaching and tutoring, in which learning happens as flashes of insight from a joint experience rather than by force-feeding or imposition from above. This particular supervisor conceived of his task as alliance and vigilance, promoting learning from experience by discussion of clinical material, and transmitting his own enthusiasm for the subject matter. He stressed that the attention to a third, 'the client's problem' was the focus of supervision as well as of therapy (Holt, 1976), and that this was always embedded in a field of unconscious forces which were not to be taken lightly. When he spoke of libido or transference these words sounded like the mysteries fuelling all human relating, be it personal or professional, and even the word 'resistance' was mentioned with the respect due to a life-enhancing energy that needs to be gone with rather than be broken or dismissed.

He taught us the meaning of symptoms and the importance of dreams as roads into psychic complexities beyond plain words and demonstrated how to be attentive to the clinical detail of our client's narratives without getting stuck in their concreteness or showing prurience when secrets and sensitive issues were revealed. He was always interested to know how we felt about the clients and speculated with us how they might perceive us, drawing on a vast repertoire of his own cases and teaching us the Masters with awe and gratitude. One never felt harshly criticised or humiliated when one had made a blunder or showed ignorance about something, and much self-doubt disappeared when he demonstrated how clients could get one to do things unwittingly. In my case it was an anxious moment when my first client asked me whether I was a trainee and I instantly said 'no'. This, he said, was what she wanted me to say in order to feel safe. It was an inspired way of teaching the power of unconscious projection and amounted to the induction into a craft that seemed difficult as well as rewarding and demanded a strange amalgam of intuition, intelligence and attention to detail, which he himself possessed and demonstrated indefatigably, making therapy and supervision seem eminently worthwhile, necessary and life-enhancing.

His example inspired me to become a supervisor and, carried along by the force of positive transference, I discovered an aptitude if not a vocation for supervision which I have since come to consider a blessing. For me, the emotional experience of identification with my supervisor and of my supervisor's modelling of the therapeutic attitude laid the foundations simultaneously for therapy and for supervision, transmitting the shared ethos and values of a profession which requires its practitioners to have both, mandatorily throughout their extensive training, and then by choice throughout the rest of their professional career. It seems to be a special form of object-relating in the presence of and with another, similar to teaching, to parenting and to creative thinking. When there is the experience of understanding certain life processes, these can be profoundly influenced and altered by joint thinking about them in the therapeutic or supervisory space, and conversely they will be having a self-altering effect on the observer, as well as on the observed.

Supervision is always transformation and metamorphosis. It has been described as an experiential form of learning and teaching, and this is certainly true when the powerful element of therapeutic action affecting all three participants in the exercise is taken into account. My own experience of supervision was first in a training context, where it was flanked by personal therapy and by my first supervised attempts at counselling clients. In this tripartite scenario I was receiving and giving simultaneously, and was experiencing myself in three different roles, as well as participating in seminars and experiential groups. It amounted to total immersion in a therapeutic world and this happens to everybody who is training to be a psychotherapist. It is an intensive learning environment in which therapy is the subject of thinking, experiencing and practising by the same person. She may feel pushed and pulled in many directions mentally, emotionally and spiritually so that everything is put into question and requires answers.

If it wasn't for supervision, trainees might disintegrate, go mad, get lost in the maze of new impressions, drown in the wealth of new information, or panic for lack of sufficient capacity to take in, process and assimilate all they are confronted with. Supervision becomes the place – either in a one-to-one or in a group situation – where the welter of new impressions and ideas can be gathered, anchored and reflected on and where some integration of feeling and thinking can eventually be achieved. It will have a containing function because the supervisor will attend to the task of facilitating the therapist's learning to be with the patient and will enable him or her to develop the ability to perform the three roles: of patient (in their personal therapy), therapist (with their training patients) and supervisee (while thinking about their patients' clinical material in supervision). All three roles make up the competent and effective therapist who will hopefully emerge from the arduous training ready to practise their new profession, in private practice or in the context of an organisation, such as the NHS, education, or business and industry.

I have stressed the interconnection of therapy, supervision and clinical practice during psychotherapy training, because there is something uniquely formative in this combination of thinking, doing and reflecting on theory, self and practice, which miraculously and creatively brings about the desired professional integration and equips the trainee with self-awareness, theoretical knowledge and practical skill. A considerable amount of supervised practical work is undertaken in the course of training, parallel to acquiring the necessary body of theory, therapeutic technique and management skills under the guidance of experienced practitioners who conscientiously assess the trainees' aptitude and performance until they are satisfied that they have reached the ethical standards of practice expected of graduates and can be trusted to implement what they have learnt and demonstrated in supervision. The supervisor hence takes personal responsibility for the supervisees' professional readiness and acts as their mentor and guarantor on entering the profession.

This is an awesome task of putting one's belief into someone one may hardly know, but as it is usually shouldered by more than one person it is less burdensome than it sounds. Fortunately, in most cases it is relatively straightforward as the assessment is ongoing over some years and therefore decisions are usually relatively unanimous. Except when there are niggling doubts as to a candidate's reliability and trustworthiness which may have always been there and might have something to do with the level of pathology in the candidate which may not have shifted in their ongoing therapy as the selector may have hoped at their initial interview.

A certain degree of psychic disturbance in a candidate is inevitable as only people with sensitivity to and personal experience of emotional crises are likely to be attracted to this difficult and demanding work of engaging with others around their emotional dilemmas. The existence of pathology in candidates is a dilemma facing selector and assessor at the beginning and end of training when they have to weigh the evidence of manageable neurotic states against possibly destructive pathological traits; and the latter may eventually make them decide against a candidate's admission into the profession. This also bedevils supervision when in the course of working together there are signs of serious deterioration in the client which escape the counsellor and have been neglected or misinterpreted out of ignorance, defensiveness or inexperience. Then the supervisor must temporarily act decisively, give clear instructions on what to do, insist on their own reading of events and suggest strategies of tackling the situation. In fact, she will use her authority and temporarily take on the clinical responsibility for the client in order to save the situation. This is a scenario with which every supervisor needs to be able to engage speedily and by right of the role. In fact, if the supervision is consistently attentive, dangerous developments can usually be foreseen and forestalled before they develop into crises, and such foresight, born of vigilance and extensive experience of clinical work, is the hallmark of good supervision.

The decision to turn down candidates is made on the basis of their ongoing clinical work. How this has developed and progressed over time, as well as the quality of their therapeutic relationships, the outcome of their therapy and the matching of goals and achievements will be carefully assessed against certain general criteria and all this together with their own assessment of their performance will decide the verdict of their suitability. Of greatest importance is the development of an analytic attitude, of healthy professional self-confidence, firm professional boundaries and personal stability that guarantee candidates a relatively easy integration into the existing professional body. They also need sufficient initiative to develop a career of their own and the ability to gain the trust of their patients. 'Would I refer her a client or would I refer myself to her for therapy?' is the question that eventually needs to be asked and answered in the affirmative before a candidate can be admitted into the fold (Plaut, 1982). I maintain that this question will need to be asked periodically as therapists carry on working and it is only through ongoing conscientious supervision that it can be kept alive, and through the continuing vigilance of the whole profession with regard to its ethical standards and the expectations placed in its members.

As a supervisor one is often asked to provide references for present or former supervisees and this is a very responsible task when it might involve an important career move or a life-stage decision requiring a change of direction. It takes a diplomatic use of language to indicate that a strength may also be a weakness, and an intuitive ability is absolutely essential to foresee the development of potential into actuality, or what is commonly called the blossoming factor. How much weight these recommendations carry is generally difficult to gauge, but a balanced and honest account is certainly more useful to a future employer than are eulogies or anxious warnings. It is very gratifying when a supervisee fulfills one's expectations by doing well in the profession and there is a distinct condition which I would like to call supervisor's pride, comparable to parent's pride when their offspring is doing well.

On the whole supervision is a subtle form of influencing akin to the teacher's formative role and can be seen as a blend of identification, internalisation, imitation and competition which repeats the growth and assimilation processes operative between parents and children from the early developmental stages. The obvious theoretical model is Winnicott's concept of the potential space (1971): the psychic overlap between mother and child which allows for satisfying communication, profound experiences of mutuality, and, ultimately, for the creation of learning processes which carry over into adult life and into our encounters with others. Of psychotherapy he wrote, 'it is done in the overlap of the two play areas, that of the patient and that of the therapist' (1971: 58). Teaching, he said, if it is to be profitable, also happens in this overlap 'Teaching aims at enrichment, yet it is an insult to indoctrinate people, even for their own good, unless they have the chance by being present to react, to express disapproval and to contribute' (1971: 58).

Today we would speak of the danger of cloning, and monitor the narcissistic temptation which a supervisor, like a teacher, has to resist particularly when working with an impressionable, perhaps idealising supervisee. There is a fine line between influence and control and it is easily crossed, when the *furor didacticus* possesses the supervisor, perhaps in response to something in the clinical material which exerts a particular fascination and invites expansive analysing in the context of theory. As with the good parent the need to rein in one's enthusiasm that might swamp and to curb bouts of verbosity that could block creative dialogue is obvious, as these spring easily from the position of authority inherent in the supervisory role of passing on expertise and experience. Equally difficult is the curbing of expectations, whether positive or negative, which as with parents and children can do much harm when the recipient is in a dependent relationship and then resorts to pleasing.

On the other hand a complementary attitude of *laissez-faire* which allows everything and praises everything in order to avoid conflict, so as to be liked and not experienced as judgemental or undermining can have equally serious effects. The recipient is then encouraged to become big-headed, omnipotent and lazy, in short narcissistic. In both cases the clients are probably not very well served, in fact, their needs may become of secondary importance to the narcissistic gratification that is obtained from talking and speculating about them and their problems. Stimmel, in a paper, 'Resistance to awareness of the supervisor's transference' points out that 'while transference reactions of the supervisee are often discussed, those of the supervisor are notably missing in our literature' (1995: 609) particularly when they involve pleasure and positive feelings in the supervisory relationship. It then becomes 'an enactment between supervisor and supervisee and is thus ripe with possibilities for disguise, displacement and gratification' (1995: 609). Consider the case of a supervisee who was her supervisor's favourite. The supervisor was rather lax on boundaries, loved the sound of her own voice, was keen to socialise outside sessions and, pleased with herself, brought in her own clinical material rather too readily. The supervision felt very insecure, veering between cosy and demanding, and the supervisee had great difficulties ending it when she felt she had learnt as much as she could. It was certainly not a good model to base her work on, as Langs (1994) implies, when he emphasises the importance of a secure frame, in therapy as well as in supervision.

With this statement I have come to the most important ethical imperative of supervision that determines whether it is of value, is worthwhile and well done. There are always three people in supervision of which one is absent while the other two are discussing him or her and the quality of the therapeutic relationship. The supervision will become authoritarian when the focus is on the client only, and negligent when the client is sidelined. Both activities will amount to a serious fudging of the task which needs to include all the cross-currents in the three-person field. Threesomes are notoriously difficult, as they require a sweeping or swivelling movement to become inclusive and they automatically lead to the exclusion of one or the other participant in order to simplify the situation. The supervisory perspective requires a constancy of inclusiveness which not everyone can sustain and which takes much practice before it becomes second nature. The foundation of an ethical supervisory style is the rigorous elimination of temptations to control or collude, of being prescriptive, telling off, cloning or sidelining the supervisee and/or client, all of which happens when it is done carelessly or destructively and hence not achieving its purpose of facilitating the supervisee's learning from and about the patient.

Much thought has gone into working out classifications of the roles the supervisor needs to play at various stages of the supervisee's professional development from dependence to independence and to interdependence. Sequences such as parent, teacher, tutor, mentor, colleague have been developed for this purpose (Stoltenberg and Delworth, 1987). There has also been an interesting attempt to classify supervisees' learning and thinking styles coupled with advice on how to respond to these judiciously and hence to adjust supervisory input accordingly (Jacobs, et al., 1995). These classifications do not go beyond schematic types which disregard the individual, nor do mnemonic slogans such as 'supervision, enabling and ensuring' nor 'formative, normative, restorative' (Proctor, 1988). One cannot forget Ekstein and Wallerstein's inspired coinage for the two main learning problems in supervision, the attention to 'blind spots' (denial) and 'dumb spots' (ignorance).

Doing supervision over many years teaches one learns to trust one's intuition and to treat every individual supervisory relationship as unique, whether with trainees or with experienced therapists. This means practising what Daniel Stern (1985) called 'attunement' when he spoke of the mother's response to her baby's affective needs. This 'intersubjective relatedness', to use another concept of Stern's, is the foundation of any interaction or dialogue, and of seeing these as unique and different with each person and dependent on many subtle processes going on between two people who are communicating feeling or thinking states. Intuition plays a large part in this intersubjectivity, as do each partner's guessing attempts at getting the other right, and at understanding how they organise reality or defend against it.

When we speak of the trainee/therapist's development of a 'professional self' in supervision as distinct from the 'personal self' which is developed in therapy it is very useful to think of Stern's various self-states which he identified as developing consecutively in infancy: the emergent self, the core self, the subjective self, and the verbal self. The beginner's professional self is vulnerable in its early encounters with client and supervisor, and the latter's attunement to the supervisee who is taking the first steps with the client needs to be sensitive, offering containment of anxiety, facilitation of rapprochement and rapport, and a firm offer of supportive listening. The first presentations of clinical material may still be in the form of raw material rather than organised narrative and will be offered expectantly to the supervisor for enlightening comment, shaping and understanding. 'Holding the therapeutic couple' is essentially a task of 'being with another' who is relating to a stranger while encountering the first client with whom he or she will learn the rudiments of being a therapist.

Every person will go about this in a different way and the supervisor, while gathering important first impressions, will be attuning to it in a correspondingly unique way. It requires an effort to establish the beginnings of a learning relationship that can be helpful and formative to the emergent self, allowing dependence, imitation, anxiety management, curiosity and primitive conceptualising. In a nutshell, all three participants will be experiencing something similar, though with varying degrees of intentionality, understanding and self-consciousness, connecting with another for the joint therapeutic enterprise. The supervision will navigate carefully through the unfolding processes by focusing, structuring and reflecting. Sensitive attunement and playback is crucial for the supervisor to start off this process of induction and achieve a matching of personal styles to get something going without undue anxiety that can become creative and facilitate the learning about and from the patient which is essential for the therapeutic work.

There is thus constant attunement to both relationships, the therapeutic and the supervisory, and often there are similarities or parallel processes which arise from the juxtaposition or mingling of the two relationships in the therapist's unconscious, and the presentation and the consecutive discussion of clinical material. As the supervisee is unconsciously affected by the patient, so the supervisor is unconsciously affected by the supervisee needing to grasp the interaction of many forces and personalities, noting without necessarily verbalising the intricate intermingling of anxieties, expectations and feelings that is enriched with incipient transference and counter-transference experiences by each couple.

My proposition is that every piece of supervision, like a primary relationship, will start off with unique experiences of attunement which will shape the course of things to come and lay down the matrices of ensuing relationships. Much of this is intuitive, tentative and unconscious, yet it is essentially determined by the supervisor's willingness to stage a skilful entry into each relationship, tailored to every individual's needs, characteristics and circumstances. As the supervisee's professional self-states unfold and develop – core self following emergent self and leading to subjective self – he or she will demand adjustments to the attunement in line with subtly different demands and expectations and the supervisory relationship will alter, becoming more or less relaxed according to the quality of the supervisee's learning experience while working with clients and presenting this work to the supervisor for inspection, advice and approval.

Some therapists falter in the early stages of the supervisory relationship, when there is a bad fit, a fear of or resistance to the task and when there is the realisation that the sense of self is too weak to persist. Early dropouts are unavoidable and it is painful for all concerned to acknowledge that the supervision has miscarried soon after it started for lack of aptitude, interest or firmness of purpose, and that the supervisory attunement did not lead to a prospering relationship. Those who cross the threshold, however, and enter the stage of professional core selfhood will increasingly demonstrate in their working and relating, the growth of self-agency, self-coherence, self-affectivity and self-history, to use Stern's (1985) categories. This indicates that the supervisee is acquiring a stronger sense of professional self to which the supervisor can attune in a more robust and challenging way and which he or she can rely on to relate to his interventions creatively and idiosyncratically.

The experienced supervisee's therapeutic work will continue to need no less attunement and vigilance from the supervisor, but it will develop more independently from instruction and will assume in their presentation the dimension of an organised narrative that reflects the supervisee's understanding of what is going on and where the process is leading. In moments of getting stuck, impasse or confusion, instead of fear and panic, there can be joint reflection, the unravelling of knots or the exploration of individual or mutual blind spots which indicate that supervisee and client might have become unconsciously identified, using projection and other defences to avoid painful consciousness.

There may also have to be a patient waiting for the arrival of insight in one or the other participant, and the calm enduring of 'uncertainties, mysteries, doubts without any irritable reaching for facts and reason' (John Keats, in a letter to his brothers, December 1817) which is a vital ingredient of psychotherapy when the participants have reached the necessary maturity. The development of a professional core self in supervision depends largely on the ability to learn from experience, guided and enriched by the wider professional experience of the supervisor who remains attuned at every step of the process to the supervisee's growing knowledge and skill which enables him or her to gauge how much input and comment is needed to optimally facilitate the therapeutic relationship.

At this stage two further self stages described by Stern can be observed in the supervisee which require acknowledgement and validation. These are the subjective self which facilitates the 'sharing of affect' and promotes empathy, and the verbal self which allows 'the sharing of different world knowledge between self and other, mutual experiences of meaning and an augmentation of interpersonal experience' (1985: 162), in short, a sophisticated supervisory dialogue around the clinical material.

Stern described the development of a sense of self as an 'experential integration'. It follows that the development of a professional sense of self is the ultimate aim of supervision which allows the practitioner to reach a professional integration that in turn will facilitate the patient's desired psychic integration and hence further the ultimate goal of psychotherapy.

Supervision, based on an intuitive attunement to the therapist's unfolding learning needs and professional self-experiences promotes and fine-tunes a therapist's ability to become and to remain attuned to her patients, in a process of modelling herself on the supervisor who could be described as performing a parental task. It is difficult to go into detail and to explain the full complexity of what happens when supervisor and supervisee meet to discuss the patient, and it remains mysterious to some extent how such discussions can influence what happens in the next session between the two therapeutic partners. But mostly something gets transmitted that helps the therapist to a better understanding and the patient to a shifting of positions and to change due to feeling better understood and more firmly held. Unless, of course, there is resistance and anxiety in one or the other that blocks the supervisory channel and snuffs out the creative spark.

As Stimmel (1995) observed, resistance is not unique to the patient, nor to the supervisee. The supervisor, too, develops resistance when attunement becomes blunted or when strong feelings of love and hate obstruct the attentive neutrality that is necessary to practise attunement consistently. As there are three participants, each with their unique psychopathology, the vicissitudes of supervision are infinite and require constant careful monitoring and vigilance. In the past, supervisors concentrated on the patient's progress and considered the supervisees only when they showed signs of ineptitude, interfered harmfully in the patient's progress or perpetrated obvious verbal blunders. Breaking of boundaries and negligence in holding the analytic frame were always considered unethical and unprofessional. But there was neglect of their own process to the detriment of the task and for fear of becoming therapeutic. This deprived them of important therapeutic tools like their own counter-transference and the correct identification of reflection processes which Searles (1965) was the first to notice and use creatively in his analytic supervising. Formerly, thus, the supervisory relationship was bracketed out and it took some time before the full dynamic interplay of unconscious forces that make up the rich tapestry of supervision could be acknowledged. Every participant in the exercise in fact stays enfolded in an analytic system that encourages and enhances self-reflection and eventually will achieve this purpose when the participants are able to sustain high levels of awareness and attunement to the fluctuating self-states.

One further legitimate function of supervision beyond the point of having established a well-functioning professional self is the consultation among equals and experienced therapists which serves the maintenance and sustenance of ongoing therapeutic practice. Increasingly, practitioners feel the need for continuing supervision beyond graduation and seek out a supervisory case discussion when they require a second opinion or hope to be extracted from an intractable impasse. Opening the 'closed vessel' of the dyad to a third and inviting comment may seem risky and exposing when the situation is barely articulable and has so far escaped conceptualisation. Actually it is valiant attempt to put into words what has seemed ineffable and to express the complexity of feelings accompanying a scenario that cannot be understood. It will usually lead to some form of resolution, particularly when the consultant supervisor is able to ask the right questions, to jog the therapist's thinking into making new links and associations and to remember significant detail that was overlooked.

More often than not the cause is an unacknowledged erotic transference or denial of envious feelings, but a secret fear of breakdown can also block the therapeutic process until it is admitted and shared. When Freud compared the analytic process to detective work he found an inspired simile, also for the supervisory task, particularly at an advanced level, when the linking of material from various sources like memories, dreams, reconstructions of past events and counter-transference experiences feels as if one is assembling a puzzle from the discrete pieces offered by the patient in no chronological order, or, to change the metaphor, when one needs to find a radically different way of telling the life story which includes vital clues so far withheld.

I am thinking of a piece of supervision with a very experienced colleague who had been working for years with a patient with a stubborn resistance to expressing herself verbally who showered him with pictures and dreams that refused to make sense and that became another obfuscating defensive manoeuvre. Eventually we found the missing clues in the suicide of the patient's brother that had happened years ago, but which she had not been able to face until the therapist remembered in supervision a significant dream from the beginning of the therapy. That somehow enabled the patient to find her voice and finally to develop a verbal self that led her to creatively read her life story as an ongoing journey which she would be able to continue by herself.

Supervisory experiences like this are not only conclusive proof of the value of psychotherapy, but they also amount to a full justification of the value of supervision. In the course of this particular supervision we became very creative together, finding myths, paintings and images that illuminated our intricate search and exploration of the rich material and helped us piece together the fragmentary story until it made sense. We also noted with surprise how much each of us learnt about ourselves that had not been covered in our analyses, and how much new insight we gained for our craft, for the understanding of its theories and of the complicated ways in which psychic processes develop and get worked through. Though it took nine years for this woman to come fully alive, to become liberated from the burden of her brother's suicide and from her oppressive childhood, and one year of supervision to implement the final rescue, it seemed eminently worthwhile.

In conclusion: supervision is an amazingly interesting, complex and rewarding activity, and its power to uncover, transform and enrich is almost unlimited. When it is done on the level of the last example with an experienced practitioner it can have the miraculous effect of profound metamorphosis, for the therapist as well as for the patient. The supervisor becomes a 'transformational object', to use Christopher Bollas' (1979) inspired concept. Though rarely credited with this in the clinical literature and difficult to pin down in individual cases, its contribution to therapeutic outcome as much as to the professional formation of therapists is incalculable. And finally it contributes significantly to the maintenance of ethical standards in the profession and to the overall value of psychotherapy.

References

Bollas, C. (1979) 'The transformational object', *International Journal of Psycho-Analysis*, 60: 97–107.

Holt, D. (1976) *Some Aspects of Supervision*, WPF Counselling and Psychotherapy Guide no. 3. London: WPF Counselling and Psychotherapy.

Jacobs, D., David, P. and Meyer, D.J. (1995) *The Supervisory Encounter*. New Haven, CT and London: Yale University Press.

Keats, J. (1817) in R. Gittings (ed.) (1970) *Letters of John Keats*. New York: Oxford Paperbacks.

Langs, R. (1994) *Doing Supervision and Being Supervised*. London: Karnac.

Mattinson, J. (1975) *The Reflection Process in Casework Supervision*. London: Tavistock Institute.

Plaut, A. (1982) 'How do I assess progress in supervision?', *Journal of Analytical Psychology*, 24(4), pp. 107–110.

Proctor, B. (1988) 'Supervision: a co-operative exercise in accountability', in M. Marken and M. Payne (ed.), *Enabling and Ensuring, Supervision in Practice*. Leicester: National Youth Bureau. pp. 24.

Rioch, M. (1980) 'The dilemmas of supervision in dynamic psychotherapy', in A.K. Hess (ed.), *Psychotherapy Supervision: Theory, Research, and Practice*. New York: John Wiley. pp. 68–77.

Searles, H.F. (1965) 'The informational value of the supervisor's emotional experiences' in: *Collected Papers on Schizophrenia and Related Subjects*. London: Maresfield Library.

Stern, D. (1985) *The Interpersonal World of the Infant, A View from Psychoanalysis and Developmental Psychology*. New York: Basic Books.

Stimmel, B. (1995) 'Resistance to the awareness of the supervisor's transferences with special reference to the parallel process' *International Journal of Psycho-Analysis*, 76(6): 609–618.

Stoltenberg, C.D. and Delworth, U. (1987) *Supervising Counselors and Therapists. A Developmental Approach*, San Francisco and London: Jossey-Bass.

Winnicott, D.W. (1971) *Playing and Reality*. London: Tavistock.

Chapter 4

Internal States in the Supervisory Relationship

Christine Driver

In supervision the psychic manifestation of the patient's material is reflected within the intensity of the relationship with the supervisor which itself has many different levels and domains. Understanding the processes in supervision requires an awareness of unconscious processes and unconscious identifications. Working with this therapeutically, within supervision, requires an ability to hold an awareness of the unconscious dynamics of supervision while interpreting through the supervisory axis to the clinical axis with the patient. The historical developments of supervision reflect the dilemmas inherent in this process. As outlined in Chapter 1 the Hungarian model advocated supervision within the therapist's own analysis so that the therapist's own treatment could be used to 'explore his [the therapist's] relationship with his patient and thus obtain a deeper understanding of his own resistances and difficulties in conducting analytic work', and it was considered that, 'It was with his analyst that the candidate could have the most open and far-reaching discussion of his reactions to his patient and their origins'. (Jacobs et al., 1995: p 20–21, my parenthesis). In about 1935, however, the 'representatives of the Institute of Vienna' (Ekstein and Wallerstein, 1972) proposed that supervision of clinical work needed to be separated and differentiated from the therapist's analysis and that 'the candidate . . . should work with a person who would teach him rather than analyse him' (1972: p 244). This separation was important in that it placed a boundary between therapy and supervision and enabled the therapist to have a different input in relation to the clinical work, but there was also a sense in which the baby was thrown out with the bath water. Supervision subsequently veered towards a supervisory dyad and a didactic process. The focus was on the patient and the 'informational value' of the supervisor's and supervisee's transference and counter-transference responses were marginalised. In 1955, Searles (1986) in his paper 'The informational value of the supervisor's emotional experience' linked together the fundamental components of both these models. His concept of the reflection process brought together the importance of counter-transference, unconscious communication, process and the supervisory relationship. He developed an understanding of how the unconscious processes of the patient and of the patient in relation to the therapist are reflected in the supervisory process and the therapist's relationship with the supervisor. The importance of Searles' paper, and of papers by Mattinson (1975), Ekstein and Wallerstein (1972) and others on the reflection and parallel processes, is that they deepen and develop our understanding of what happens when two people meet and work together either as patient and therapist or as therapist and supervisor. As Andrew Samuels comments, 'Depth psychology is less about "things" than about the relations between things, and ultimately about the relations between sets of relations. Impact at one point of the psychic system leads to ripples through the whole apparatus' (1989: 9).

The dilemma of the supervisory process is that there are factors which a supervisor needs to be aware of but to abstain from. In therapy, abstinence primarily relates to acting out within the therapeutic relationship as well as to refraining from sadistically attacking the patient with 'interpretations' that fail to take into account their 'triangle of conflict' (Malan, 1979). Similarly in supervision, and especially one-to-one supervision, the supervisor must respect the privacy of the supervisee's internal world and abstain from stepping into a relationship with it. On the other hand the supervisor must work with the supervisee to overcome blind spots and dumb spots and enable reflection on any parallel and reflection processes. The supervisor has to hold a tension in relation to the supervisee to enable the holding of a creative space in their internal world that will help the supervisee to relate to what is caught up in the projections and transferences of the patient. This tension is an integration of the two original models of supervision and reflects the development of a complex process whereby the supervisor needs to recognise but contain the ambiguous/dual nature of supervision and the supervisory relationship. The dynamic within supervision of both intimacy and abstinence, and the inherent frustrations, potentially creates a mental space in which the observing ego (Greenson, 1981) of the supervisee can develop. Before I go on to consider this in more detail, however, I want to look at the various elements of the supervisory relationship within one-to-one supervision.

The supervisory alliance

The initial determining factors of the supervisory relationship are the setting in which the supervision takes place and the clinical rhombus (Ekstein and Wallerstein, 1972) in which it is contained. The setting will determine the type and style of work, the demands on the supervisor and supervisee and the various parameters to which both will have to attend e.g., patient fees, length of work, demands of training, etc. From the start therefore both supervisor and supervisee are affected by the setting. Even in private practice the frame and setting of the clinical work and supervision will have an effect both on the patient and the supervisee. The setting therefore needs to contain the needs of the patient and the supervisee and reflect a framework that is 'safe' and professional. Usually individual supervision lasts for 50 minutes, the supervisee brings clinical work to the supervisor and, as in any relationship where there are elements of need and dependency, there will be transference, anxiety and possibly regression. This is most clearly evident in any training organisation but needs to be recognised in settings where there are defined, and necessary, hierarchies, or clear staff distinctions e.g., between voluntary counsellors and paid supervisors.

The 50-minute supervisory session provides a container that parallels and mirrors the frame of the therapeutic setting. But what are the consequences? Perhaps the main value is that it allows the possibility for the supervisor and supervisee to experience what it is like to be with the patient(s). It allows a clear and intense focus on a piece of work which is contained within the setting and a parallel space in which the supervisee can experience how to understand the clinical material and develop their way of working. The paralleling of the setting allows a greater potential for parallel process and hence an experience of the patient's internal world. However if we accept that in one-to-one supervision there is a paralleling of the therapeutic frame then we must take notice of how the therapeutic relationship affects the supervisory one. Langs (1994) clearly refers to this when he talks about frame deviations and alterations of the frame and how they may affect the unconscious processes between supervisee and patient. An effective supervisory alliance will therefore respect the frame of the process, and the relationship within it, in a way in which both the frame and the relationship enable the supervisee to define the work.

Once we have taken into account the parameters of the setting we need to consider the fundamental issue of orientation and supervisory alliance. The supervisory alliance is more than just a contract to work together; it requires both parties to be able to orientate themselves to a frame of reference where each can understand the other in an internal way as well as an external one, i.e. where 'the words' have a meaning that conveys emotional understanding. In any 'work' based relationship there needs to be mutual elements of respect, co-operation and collaboration in a process of exploration and discovery. Doubtless there will be anxiety and dependency, especially in a training situation, but there needs to be a willingness in the supervisee to engage in a process which is fundamentally about exploration. Supervisees, especially those new to the profession, often come with the hope of being taught 'how to do it'. The supervisor in this instance needs to hold the dependency needs, but also engage with the supervisee at an adult ego level that enables a development of the professional self to explore, reflect and listen to the transference and counter-transference feelings and make links and observations to the patient's internal conflicts and internal world. Supervisors need to foster desires in supervisees to engage in an ego related process of observation and understanding so as to enable supervisees to experience themselves as a tool with which to monitor the patient's experience of himself and his internal world. The supervisor then engages with the supervisee's observing ego to enable them to develop their own 'internal supervisor' (Casement, 1985). This is very succinctly put by Jacobs et al. (1995):

> A psychotherapist needs to learn from the dialogue with his supervisor how to contain and interpret his own feelings, at least to the degree that these feelings are relevant to the therapy. Supervision must not only accommodate a dialogue about the trainee's affective experiences in doing treatment but also teach the skills that eventually equip therapists to identify, contain, and analyse affective experiences on their own. The educational implication is that students should acquire some facility with self-reflection and self-analysis as part of their psychotherapy curriculum. (1985: 143)

The aim of supervision therefore is to create a working partnership in which the development of the work with the patient and the development of the supervisee's professional abilities takes place simultaneously. We are therefore aiming at a development within the supervisee of a movement from a dependent state at the beginning of clinical work to a more independent and self reflective state as experience develops (Stoltenberg and Delworth, 1987).

The importance of a supervisor viewing the supervisee as a junior colleague (Fordham, 1961) is essential if the supervisee is going to be enabled by the supervisory process to develop their clinical ability. Supervision is therefore, to use Fordham's phrase, a 'deintegrative process' through which the observing/reflective ego of the supervisor engages and encourages the potential observing/reflective ego in the supervisee. The willingness to engage in this process is the underpinning of a supervisory alliance which allows growth and development in the work and in the supervisee.

Alliance, authority and process

We need to view supervision, and especially one-to-one supervision, as more than an enabling process in which development takes place. The supervisor needs to have a sense of their own authority and to use it wisely so as to be able to challenge the supervisee and make appropriate assessments. Within the supervisory alliance the supervisor holds a tension between authority, expertise, theory, assessment, anxiety, exploration and not knowing. It is perhaps even more important to recognise this in one-to-one supervision than in group supervision as the unconscious processes may disable both supervisor and supervisee from being able to think critically about the patient's material. There is therefore a tension inherent in the supervisory process. On the one hand the supervisor is working within a process which enables discovery and, on the other, is needing to maintain their own observing ego and hold an authority that emanates from experience and expertise. As in all balancing acts there is, inevitably, a danger of collapse to either extreme. For example a didactic supervisor might use the power of their role and function in such a way that it is persecutory or unhelpful to the supervisee. While on the other hand a supervisor who is unable to utilise their objective authority and ability to assess is failing both the patient and the supervisee.

A relatively new counsellor brought to supervision a piece of work where she described the patient as very distressed following two bereavements. The patient's material contained clear references to suicidal thoughts but the counsellor had failed to respond to this. As the supervisee presented in supervision I became aware that I was also not responding to the suicidal anxiety presented in the material. The anxiety provoked by the patient's material was causing both myself and the supervisee to unconsciously identify with the despair. Having become aware of this I was able to explore with the supervisee how she was colluding with the patient in defending against the feelings of loss and despair and was failing to address the suicidal thoughts. In consequence we were able to make a clear assessment of the patient's emotional state and needs, and outline the focus the supervisee's work with the patient needed to take.

In this fairly obvious example it is clear that I, as supervisor, would have 'failed' the supervisee and the patient if I had also got caught in colluding with the denial. But it illustrates the need for the supervisor to be both inside and outside the supervisory relationship simultaneously, that is to be both subjective and objective. This means sometimes being didactic and wisely asserting authority in the interests of the patient and the supervisee. A working alliance therefore depends as much on the internal attitude of the supervisor as it does on that of the supervisee. Even beginning supervisees need a willingness to learn and understand (Hawkins and Shohet, 1989) so that their own egos are placed in a position in which they can process and reflect on the thoughts and feelings which emanate from the patient and from the re-experiencing of these within supervision. A supervisor, especially in one-to-one work, needs to encourage and enable processes of reflection within the supervisee. The supervisor needs to aim to be a navigator who points out the co-ordinates and constituents of the work so as to enable the supervisee to define the transference, counter-transference and projections and to make links to the internal states from which the patient is relating.

Transference and counter-transference in supervision

When therapists choose a supervisor or have one chosen for them, what are the parameters that influence that choice? What are the internal mental states and internal agendas with which the supervisee comes to supervision? These are questions that are asked when a potential patient is being assessed for clinical work but it is equally important to be mindful of the unconscious or conscious factors that underpin the one-to-one supervisory relationship. When someone comes for individual supervision, whether independently or as a requirement of their organisation, factors relating to the personality of both supervisor and supervisee will be a part of the equation into which the clinical work is brought. As a supervisor I am aware that I have been ideal-ised, hated, envied, feared and loved, and maybe other things besides, and I am aware that the supervisory relationship can never be entirely free of trans-ference, projection and regression. In group supervision the projections and transferences extend within the matrix of the group but in individual supervi-sion there is an intense matrix of interactions into which the clinical work is being brought. These projections, transferences, anxieties and regressions may act as vehicles for the reflection process but they may also need to be held and understood in their own right.

Supervision therefore has a dual nature, one spoken and one unspoken, one personal and one professional but where the personal is held (largely) unspoken within the professional. This relationship in which, to a greater extent, the personal is abstained from but held in relation to the professional, activates and creates a developmental and Oedipal challenge for both super-visor and supervisee. The internal mental states and the internal agendas with which a supervisee comes to supervision are contained within the external agenda of supervision. This is as true for group supervision as it is for one-to-one supervision but I wish to explore this within the parameters of one-to-one supervision because here these issues are contained in a potentially much more powerful way.

As a supervisor my aim is to enable the supervisee to define the work with the patient in terms of unconscious processes, projections, transference and counter-transference, latent and symbolic meanings of the content of the ses-sions, and appropriate ways of working with these within the relationship with the patient. I need to consider this in relation to the level of experience of the supervisee. If they are relatively new to working as a counsellor or therapist I will need to consider how I enable them to define the work themselves so that the process of supervision becomes part of their own internal process, i.e. how they begin to formulate their own 'internal supervisor' (Casement, 1985) and 'observing ego' (Greenson, 1981). However this formulation of supervision makes a basic assumption. It assumes that the relationship between supervi-sor and supervisee occurs on a fundamentally adult-to-adult level and does not take into account the undercurrents of emotional and mental states which occur within the supervisee and alongside the supervisory process. No super-visee comes to a new supervisor 'cold', i.e. without some kind of anticipatory fantasy or expectation. We may ask ourselves, 'why have they chosen that supervisor, why now, what are the expectations?' Is there a hope and an ex-pectation of what they will gain, a hope that supervisors will feed them the rich milk of their insights and expertise? In a profession which generates hier-archies it is difficult to escape these projections and the ramifications in terms of hopes, expectations, anxiety and regression.

A supervisee who came to me for individual supervision had clearly chosen me because I was established in the therapeutic profession. What soon became clear however was that she hoped to adhesively identity with me, and that her knowl-edge that I was 'established' fuelled a fantasy that she was 'established'. Her internal omnipotence was apparent and was mirrored by a training which expected trainees to set up their own counselling practice to gain clinical experience for the training. It immediately became apparent through what she brought, and didn't bring, to supervision that I had to take a stance to confront her omnipotence and enable her to face her lack of experience and of what she needed to put into place to be able to work ethically and effectively. In this case therefore I needed to use my awareness of her personal transference to me as supervisor to inform myself of the primary issues of competence, responsibility to the patient and ethics, and that the working alliance had to be forged at this level so as to confront the issues involved.

In some ways the transference manifestations in this particular case reflected elements of the states found in any beginner counsellor or therapist who is new to the work. Stoltenberg and Delworth (1987) and Hawkins and Shohet (1989) outline the states prevalent in a 'level 1' trainee as dependent, imitative, anxious and highly motivated. This was certainly the case with my supervisee who, in her anxiety, wanted to identify with me and was dependent on me, but within this there were other aspects to the personal equation which reflected her own material, and this was reflected in her manner and attitude, in the transference and in her reasons for coming to me as a supervisor.

Intimacy and abstinence

In the above example the supervisee's internal fantasy and projection were obvious but with most supervisees it is not necessarily clear as to why they have chosen to come to you for supervision. However the therapist within the supervisor is almost certain to get a glimpse of this internal agenda and of the supervisee's internal emotional state. This is where the supervisor walks a tightrope between intimacy in relation to the work with the patient and abstinence in terms of the supervisee's own personal 'work'. This juxtaposition of intimacy and abstinence is also part of the developmental process for the supervisee. Many new therapists are highly dependent on the supervisor and may form an adhesive identification. Supervisors need to enable supervisees to develop their ways of thinking and processing the patient material so that supervisees are able to develop their own internal identity as therapists.

However even with more experienced supervisees the presence of transference, projection, and fantasy will almost inevitably be present. Whatever the internal and transference agendas of the supervisee the supervisor needs to always 'fail' it, i.e. hold the frame on the supervisory work so that the supervisee cannot act out their internal fantasy. Supervision, and especially one-to-one supervision, fails and frustrates the infantile agenda and must deny the narcissistic gratification of both supervisee and supervisor. The guru cannot give the magic formula milk, the 'knowledge' cannot be found outside but has to be struggled with and integrated within. The supervisor cannot be the mother, father, lover, but may hold that role in the transference for the supervisee.

The fact that the supervisor 'fails' the supervisee in this respect means that the fantasy is never, and can never, be fulfilled. However the inevitable frustration is also the developmental force for the supervisee. Bion states, 'A capacity for tolerating frustration thus enables the psyche to develop thought as a means by which the frustration that is tolerated is itself made tolerable' (1967: 112). The importance of this statement is that it enables us to begin to formulate the internal processes within supervision whereby the supervisee has to develop a capacity to think and make sense of the information and sensory data that are experienced with the patient.

The supervisor and supervisee have to find a space to think and connect the patient's material to the collective base of theory and to a place where it meets the personal process of the relationship between the supervisee and the patient. It can only do that via the connection to the internal world of the supervisee and it is only through this emotional connection and a process where 'unthought thoughts' can be 'thought' about, that the supervisee can begin to enable the patient to make mutative connections. The process of 'accessing the unthinkable' has to come from within the dynamics of the supervisory relationship.

Supervision, as outlined in Chapter 1, consists of a series of pairings within a triangle but in which the patient is always the one in focus. These pairings may consist of supervisee and patient, supervisee and supervisor, or supervisor and patient but it is the patient who has to be attended to. In group supervision the projections and transferences extend within the matrix of the group and so, to some extent are more readily available for observations. In one-to-one supervision they sit intensely within the pairing and so have to be disentangled from the personal foundations of both supervisor and supervisee. Supervision is, therefore, transference loaded, i.e. transference from the patient and to a greater or lesser degree the supervisee and also the supervisor. The strength of this is that it allows the processes within supervision to occur, i.e. the personal transference from the supervisee can act as a vehicle for the transference of the personal material of the patient and as Searles (1986) reflects in his chapter 'The informational value of the supervisor's emotional experience', the supervisor's awareness of their own transference and counter-transference is part of the evidence needed to unpack the reflection process. The work, however, is in relation to the patient's material and the latent and manifest expressions of this in the transference and counter-transference responses of both supervisor and supervisee. The supervisor is therefore at the fulcrum of overlapping triangles in which the relationship with the supervisee is an endeavour to understand the patient.

One might begin to wonder whether supervision presents us with the riddle of the sphinx! In the Egyptian legend the sphinx, who was a she-monster, was born of three possible pairings. She posed the riddle to Oedipus to solve the secret of her birth but in trying to solve it Oedipus committed the crime of incest and she then slew herself. This is the riddle we must be conscious of in supervision. Jung (1956, CW 5) reflects that the riddle is a trap in which Oedipus got caught by overestimating his intellect and by the fantasy of his own omnipotence. This ancient legend reflects a cautionary tone for supervisors because we deceive ourselves if we fall into the trap of thinking we can solve all the riddles. We, like Oedipus, are in danger from our own omnipotent fantasies and inner blindness. We therefore need to be conscious of all the pairings but to abstain from the incestuous pairing with the supervisee's personal world because it would not only violate the work with the patient but would act out the unconscious wishes of the supervisee and prevent their internal development and the development of the clinical work.

The intensity and intimacy of supervision provides a tool with which to unravel the patient's material and internal world. It is also a container in which the personal elements of the relationship between the supervisor and supervisee are largely abstained from. The necessity of this is that it is only through this tension between intimacy and abstinence that a space can be created in which the patient can be experienced. What then, might be the experience of each party? If I place myself in the position of the supervisee there are various elements which I find I am holding. I have the presentation of the clinical work, I have my feelings about the patient and I have my feelings about the supervisor. In addition there are my thoughts and feelings about what the supervisor says to me about the patient and how these thoughts and feelings connect (or not) to the patient's internal world. I have to create a benign split in myself and generate an internal space in myself where I can reflect on what belongs to the patient and how I work with that as well as identifying what belongs to me, which I need to work on separately.

As a supervisor I hear the clinical material, I experience the transference and my counter-transference feelings in relation to both the material and the supervisee. I am aware of a connection between the two but also of the two independent components. I need to allude to both to elucidate the patient's dilemma but abstain from the personal aspects of the supervisee. That is, the transference and projections from the patient need to be made explicit whereas the transference from the supervisee needs to remain implicit. If we begin to work with the supervisee's transference to us as supervisors the working alliance is altered and becomes an incestuous twosome where regression is encouraged and the triangular world is lost. Regression in therapy allows for an experience and exploration of the transference. In supervision, regression by the supervisee may be present but it is not what we are wanting to encourage. Rather we are working to enable a separation and development in the supervisee of an observing ego that does not get lost in regressive yearnings but can remain able to think, link and reflect on the work with the patient.

We therefore need to view one-to-one supervision as a very powerful tool in processing the clinical material and especially so where the supervision is occuring on just one patient. One-to-one supervision generates intense and informative parallels and reflections of the patient's internal world and parental imagoes and constellates the transference and counter-transference issues within both the supervisee and the supervisor.

A male supervisee brought the case of a woman patient whose mother was a lawyer and whose father, a teacher, had taken early retirement. The supervisee expressed continued concern about his work with this patient and about how hard it was to think or verbalise the feelings in the room. He described that he often felt disabled by the patient. I found myself wanting to make didactic and formulative comments and often felt irritated and critical of the supervisee's struggle and the way he seemed to 'collapse' with this patient. When I reflected to myself on how I felt I realised that we had become polarised into two different and opposing positions and that we were both taking on aspects of the parental imagoes. Within the coupling of supervisor and supervisee the parental coupling was reflected and paralleled. The projection of the internalised parents had been split between us. I contained the critical maternal transference of 'going by the book' etc., and the supervisee contained the paternal transference of inferiority and collapse.

When I could begin to understand these dynamics and how the power of the interplay between myself and the supervisee affected our ability, or inability, to communicate I could begin to realise how the parents of the patient could not have an easy or creative verbal intercourse and of how difficult it was for the patient to experience these two opposing internal parental figures. In my interpretation to the supervisee I commented that I felt we were struggling like the patient's parents and wondered at the patient's internal conflict in relation to the internalised parents. My interpretation made use of the 'here and now' and the reflection process but interpreted through it to the patient material. This enabled reflection on the material the patient was bringing and especially the internalised aspects of the parents. It became clear to the supervisee that in the work with his patient he was dealing with the despised masculine which the patient projected on to him and with which he struggled within himself and with the patient. Alongside this the internal world of the patient was dominated by a maternal superego from which the patient was unable to successfully separate. It was apparent to me that elements of this struggle were present in the personal transference from the supervisee and maybe reflected why he had chosen me as a supervisor and why he had brought this piece of clinical work to supervision. Although the supervisory relationship contained this personal material it was my abstention from it, instead of acting into it by personalising it, that allowed the supervisee to focus on his own vulnerabilities within his own therapeutic setting. However, I, as supervisor, also needed to be aware of how aspects of my supervisory personality lay me prone to the patient's projections and the anxieties of the supervisee. I needed to utilise my ability to observe my own counter-transference to inform me of the dynamics of the work as well as to ensure that I did not collude with the projections which emanated from the patient and the supervisee. In this situation my aim was to fulfil a holding and reflecting function with the supervisee on the unconscious and clinical processes with the patient.

Montserrat Martínez del Pozo in her chapter, 'On the process of supervision in psychoanalytic psychotherapy', describes how 'learning' by the supervisee occurs when the supervisee has, 'a self with a good-enough capacity to sustain himself in the fluctuations between "integration-disintegration"' (del Pozo, 1997: 55). To contain and allow this, I had to hold on to my own anxiety in relation to the process and abstain from entering into the personal space of the supervisee, trusting that the professionalism of the supervisee would enable him to deal with this within himself or within his own therapy. By focusing on the clinical material the supervisee was able to integrate and appreciate aspects of his experience with the patient in a way that was therapeutic to his development as a therapist. The supervisee needed to develop his own internal dialogue which could separate out his personal counter-transference and transference from the projective counter-identifications (Grinberg, 1997) which emanated from the patient. Imre Szecsödy reflects:

> It was noticeable that learning did occur most frequently when the supervisor kept an equidistant position. This position is not only an open, non-judgemental, non-competitive attitude, but also includes the keeping of a continuous and stable focus on the candidate's reconstruction of his interaction with the patient: in other words, viewing the candidate-patient interaction as a 'system' with its own boundaries and frame. (Szecödy, 1997: 112)

It is in the 'internal dialogue' and in what Gee advocates as 'pondering' where, 'there is a dialogue taking place between the conscious and unconscious parts of the self' (1996: 540), that processes of integration-disintegration and de-integration-reintegration (Fordham, 1994) occur. Through this dialogue, parts of the self are brought into consciousness that, in my own experience as supervisor and supervisee, can become the mutative (and possibly therapeutic) experiences of the supervisory process. These inner mental and emotional processes may need to remain unspoken in the supervisory encounter but they form part of the internal dialogue of the supervisory process which, as Edward Martin comments in Chapter 9 of this book, 'affects the inner world and changes the inner objects of the supervisee as well as the patient'.

Conclusion

For supervision to be a mutative experience for the supervisee in relation to their understanding and ability to work with the patient's material, the supervisor must model the ego/self related activity that the supervisee needs to develop in relation to the supervisee/patient interaction. The supervisor needs to hold in their awareness that the processes of supervision have many facets within the internal world. Montserrat Martínez del Pozo's concept of the extended clinical rhombus gives us a broad framework in which to consider the parameters of the external and internal world of the supervisory process. In my examples, and in my experience as a supervisee and supervisor, the processes of supervision touch both on a 'professional self' as well as a 'personal self' (Ekstein and Wallerstein, 1972). Casement (1985: 76) defines these aspects of the internal world with his concept of the 'diagnostic response' (internal supervisor/professional self) and the 'personal countertransference' (personal self) within the supervisee. However we define these two states they can never be separated and there is, inevitably, an internal conscious or unconscious 'interactive communication' (Casement, 1985) or dialogue between the professional self and the personal self as well as interactive communication between the supervisor and aspects of the supervisee's internal world. It is these dynamics which create the potentially mutative aspect of supervision. It is inevitable that the supervisory relationship contains the personal and professional elements of both the supervisor and supervisee. It is, in part, these very elements that become the hooks for the unconscious communications from the patient. Thus, while both supervisor and supervisee have to allow themselves to be the tools of the work and to reflect on the impact of the patient's material on themselves, hidden within this is the impact that supervision can make on the internal world of the supervisee, which may itself be therapeutic.

References

Bion, W.R. (1967) *Second Thoughts*. London: Maresfield Library.

Casement, P. (1985) *On Learning from the Patient*. London: Tavistock Publications.

del Pozo, M.M. (1997) 'On the Process of Supervision in Psychoanalytic Psychotherapy' in B. Martindale et al. (eds) *Supervision and its Vicissitudes*. London: Karnac Books. pp. 39–59.

Ekstein, R. and Wallerstein, R. (1972) *The Teaching and Learning of Psychotherapy*. Madison, CT: International Universities Press, Inc.

Fordham, M. (1961) 'Suggestions Towards a Theory of Supervision' in Sonu Shamdasani (ed.) (1996) *Analyst-Patient Interaction – Collected Papers on Technique*. London: Routledge. pp. 49–56.

Fordham, M. (1994) *Children As Individuals*. London: Free Association Books.

Gee, H. (1996) 'Developing insight through supervision; relating, then defining', *The Journal of Analytical Psychology*, 41(4): 529–552.

Greenson, R.R. (1981) *The Technique and Practice of Psychoanalysis*. London: Hogarth Press.

Grinberg, L. (1997) 'On Transference and Countertransference and the Technique of Supervision' in B. Martindale et al. (eds) *Supervision and its Vicissitudes*. London: Karnac Books. pp. 1–24.

Hawkins, P. and Shohet, R. (1989) *Supervision in the Helping Professions*. Milton Keynes: Open University Press.

Jacobs, D., David P., and Meyer, D.J. (1995) *The Supervisory Encounter*. New Haven, CT and London: Yale University Press.

Jung, C.G. (1956) *Symbols of Transformation*, Collected Works, 5. London: Routledge and Kegan Paul.

Langs, R. (1994) *Doing Supervision and Being Supervised*. London: Karnac Books.

Malan, D.H. (1979) *Individual Psychotherapy and the Science of Psychodynamics*. London: Butterworth & Heinemann.

Mattinson, J. (1975) *The Reflection Process in Casework Supervision*. London: IMS/ Tavistock Institute.

Samuels, A. (1989) *The Plural Psyche*. London and New York: Routledge.

Searles, H.F. (1986) 'The Informational Value of the Supervisor's Emotional Experiences' in H.F. Searles, *Collected Papers on Schizophrenia and Related Subjects*. London: Karnac Books. pp. 157–176.

Stoltenberg, C.D. and Delworth, U. (1987) *Supervising Counselors and Therapists*. San Francisco and London: Jossey-Bass.

Szecsödy, I. (1997) '(How) is Learning Possible in Supervision?' in B. Martindale et al. (eds) *Supervision and its Vicissitudes*. London: Karnac Books. pp. 101–116.

PART II

LEARNING IN SUPERVISION

Chapter 5

The Interface Between Teaching and Supervision

John Stewart

Looking back on school days revives a mixture of remembered events and associated feelings which range from nostalgia to embarrassment. Of course we all remember the teachers, those we liked, those we feared and those to whom we were merely indifferent. Our respect for our teachers is most likely composed both of an evaluation of external factors such as how they performed in front of class and of internal factors – how they responded to us on a personal level. Different teachers inspired different pupils.

Similar reactions can be observed when psychotherapists and counsellors recall their experiences of being supervised in that some supervisors are perceived to be 'good' but others 'not so good.' The basis for such an evaluation appears to be based on a view that some have been more helpful than others or that supervisors have different strengths and weaknesses. The collective group dynamic of any organisation offering training is constantly fed by transferences and projections onto individual supervisors. I have no doubt all readers will be able to recall the expectations and anxieties raised in their own negotiations to secure supervision, let alone those situations in which they were assigned to a supervisor and, in some cases, to a supervision group.

Such anxiety is not necessarily reduced by a greater acquaintance with an organisation because the supervisee's increased exposure to the informal and collective communication systems within it can perpetuate both positive and negative reputations of individual supervisors.

Supervision implies some sort of overseeing, observation or monitoring by a person who is in a position to be partly disengaged from the activity in question. They sit to one side or hover helicopter-like above that which is being supervised – not merely as a casual observer, but in a position which assumes some authority over, or responsibility for, what is happening. The term can imply acting as mentor or guide, the assessment of performance, the maintenance of professional discipline, the ability to instruct, or the capacity to facilitate learning. A supervisor is probably all of these but listing the various facets of the role in a descriptive manner has limitations.

I intend to examine what actually happens in supervision and aspects of the process which highlight the supervisor as 'teacher'. For the sake of simplicity I will focus on the one-to-one supervisee/supervisor relationship, though the additional dynamics of group supervision are not precluded. In order to facilitate the discussion I will give a clinical example of a supervision session.

Clinical example

In order to compile the example I have drawn on my experience, but the material which follows is not an account of an actual supervision session conducted in the setting as described in the example. It is illustrative only and is included to provide a focal point to which attention may be directed in order to keep clinical activity of supervision held in mind. I will return to it from time to time as the discussion develops. My hope is that using this example may spur further thought in the reader and, as it is not an exhaustive discussion, it may well raise further questions in relation to the practice of supervison.

A female supervisor is engaged in weekly supervision in an organisational setting with an inexperienced male supervisee. The supervisee is reporting on his work with a new female patient whom he has seen weekly for three sessions and who complained, in the initial assessment session, of not being able to be creative or play. So far the sessions have been awkward and stiff encounters and the patient's demands for some 'homework' result in the therapist saying he would see what he could do about her request.

The supervisee reported a personal dream at the beginning of the fourth supervision session because he thought this may have some bearing on the interaction with his patient. The supervisee recounted a dream in which he attempted to dive into a swimming pool only to find there is a film over the surface that thwarted his attempts to have a swim. He is not sure what was happening, though he thought it may have something to do with resistance. He expressed irritation with the clinical service for giving him such a difficult patient and asked for some input from the supervisor's wide experience and reading which might help him to understand the case.

The supervisor began to reflect on the patient's statement that she was unable to play and drew attention to Winnicott's discussion on the use of creative space, the need to find the object and the development of the capacity to play. She also wondered if the dream may be drawing attention to the resistance of the therapist or to resistance being activated in the counter-transference. She encouraged the supervisee to think about this in the supervision or to discuss the matter with his therapist. The supervisee listened to the discussion and appeared to be able to reflect on the material.

In the therapy session following the supervision, the supervisee suggested to the patient that they seemed to be resisting the opportunity for therapy and commented that the patient was not able to play with the therapist. The patient attended the following session but complained that she found the therapist intrusive and said that she wished to end the therapy. The patient did not attend the next session and confirmed in writing that she had decided not to continue in counselling.

In a subsequent supervision session the supervisee expressed surprise that the patient had left as he felt he had been following the supervisor's advice. The patient did not respond to a further letter offering her time to discuss the matter further.

The supervisory triangle

Psychoanalytic or psychodynamic supervision is an activity in which the two parties – a supervisor and a supervisee, engage in thinking about previous interaction(s) between the supervisee, in the role of therapist, and the third party, the patient. The three-way or triangular nature of the relationship is complex because it is constellated in two complementary triangles. In both, two parties are engaged, while the third party, though physically absent, is present by implication. The absent patient is overtly present as the focus of discussion in the supervision session. In the therapeutic session the absent supervisor has a more covert presence, both in the awareness of the therapist and sometimes in the in the unconscious 'knowing' of the patient. Unlike the patient, the supervisor is consciously aware that they are being excluded or kept outside the interchange between the other two parties. The supervisor holds this process in mind and also assumes clinical responsibility for the work and conduct of the supervisee.

Mattinson (1975/1992) conducted research which indicated that supervisors seemed comfortable in thinking about dyadic relationships, but it proved difficult to maintain focus on the triangular dynamic of the supervisory relationship. Too often they were more articulate in describing was happening between the therapist and the patient, as related by the supervisee, but they had less recall about the process of the supervision session itself. She pointed out that the discourse of supervision is more than an act of reporting the dialogue and emotional process of the work with the patient. The supervisee's conscious recall mingles with her unconscious communication of difficulties in understanding the therapeutic process with the patient. The supervisee may bring more material to a supervision than she is consciously aware.

The therapeutic triangle and the reflection process

The manner in which the supervisee impacts on the supervisor may well unconsciously reflect or parallel the nature of the patient's impact on the supervisee. The use of the parallel or reflection process is an important aspect of the supervisor's task. It can also provide a powerful modelling experience through which the supervisee consolidates their ability to maintain the learning position, holding the dual perspective of being both participant and observer. Stimmel (1995) adds a note of caution about placing too great an emphasis on the parallel process. An apparent reflection of conflict in the patient may well mask unresolved issues in the supervisee or dissonance in the supervisory relationship.

Clinical discussion

In the clinical example I have given it seems clear that the supervisee is paralleling the patient's resistance to the therapy in the way he, as supervisee, relates to the supervisor. It is open to question where the resistance is located and more thought needs to be given to areas of personal resistance in the therapist as distinct from those reflected in the patient material. It is also worth noting that the supervisor becomes sufficiently enmeshed in the parallel process so as to give the supervisee some theory to read rather than being able to link the request for information to the patient's demand for homework.

The interface between teaching and supervision

Teaching is clearly an activity other than supervision, although supervisors have a teaching role. I want to hold the triangular focus in mind and turn again to the interface between teaching and supervision. A common aphorism is that psychodynamic supervision can be defined as an activity which is, less than personal therapy but more than teaching. This draws attention to the interface of two closely aligned therapeutic disciplines from which the activity of supervision needs to be distinguished. The supervisor faces a dual temptation in relation to the supervisee's personal needs. Too much attention can stray towards the over-indulgent and subvert the task, whilst an over-emphasis on theory or technique may drift towards sterile instruction. The supervisor grapples with the dilemma of providing sufficient support and educational input without assuming the role of therapist or teacher.

So then, how do we define the educational input of the supervisor who may at times seek clarification, challenge assumptions, give encouragement or provide theoretical input? If we return to the aphorism which describes the activity of supervision as more than teaching, we are left with the inference that supervision has common ground with, as well as differences from teaching. What do we mean by teaching? Is it the imparting of knowledge? There is a body of theoretical knowledge to be absorbed, but supervision is more than thinking or hypothesising in the abstract. Perhaps it entails giving instruction, but is supervision confined to instilling technique in supervisees? We do need theory, and technique is a vital component of the therapeutic task, but the balance is a fine one if supervisors are to avoid becoming too much like teachers.

Clinical discussion

In the example given, questions can be asked about whether the dream brings out something of the patient's resistance or is more revealing of an emotional block in the supervisee. The supervisor directed the supervisee towards further exploration in his personal therapy but was not able to explore the nature of the resistance in supervision. It may be that in drawing attention to the therapy she deflected attention from the problem at hand and her over determined attempt to avoid being the therapist could indicate that she got caught in her own resistance. The supervisor also became drawn into a teaching role when suggested that the supervisee read a paper.

Educational models and supervision

Gitterman (1977) discusses how a teacher-centred model of learning places too much reliance on the activity of teaching. The expert or teacher imparts knowledge or skill to the pupil who, as the one who is taught, is the recipient of wisdom or body of knowledge. A weakness of this approach is that learning can never advance beyond the limits of the teacher's expertise. While teachers can derive satisfaction from a demonstration of their cleverness, insufficient attention may be paid to the level of insight gained by the pupil. Indeed pupils may be criticised for being stupid or slow in their lack of understanding with little attention being paid as to why this is. Such methods tend to encourage learning by rote or assimilation of advice as a concrete set of instructions. The personality of some supervisors may cause them to adopt such a style which may collude with the more passive stance of some supervisees who wish to be instructed as to what to do.

Dickens wonderfully lampoons the dangers of a teacher-centred approach in his novel *Hard Times* (1854/1964). The teacher, Thomas Gradgrind, is described as ladling facts and more facts down the throats of neat rows of pupils. Dickens questioned the view of education that equated learning with the regurgitation of facts and competence in the art of recall. Gradgrind may be a figure of parody fit for our amusement, but it is a salutary exercise to consider those moments when, as a supervisor, we too, fall into the teacher role in an over determined manner. Of course there are times, particularly with inexperienced supervisees, when a supervisor may have to be didactic in approach and indeed there may be pressure on the supervisor to tell the supervisee what to do. If, however, the supervisee is persistently relegated to the position of a more passive participant in a didactic encounter, the effect may be to produce little more than a clone of the supervisor.

A teaching style which can be equally unhelpful is one in which the teacher abrogates the responsibility to teach anything at all. An over-permissive focus on the pupil replaces a disciplinarian emphasis on the role of the teacher. If we apply this to the teaching component in supervision, a *laissez-faire* attitude may develop, leaving the supervisee to their own devices to learn by trial and error. What learning is accomplished becomes self-directed and without significant input from the supervisor. Omnipotence thus becomes located in the supervisee rather than the supervisor and at both extremes such omnipotence can be a defence against the anxiety of not knowing.

William Golding's novel, *Lord of the Flies* (1954), is illustrative of a situation in which guidance or control is absent. A group of schoolboys, the victims of an aeroplane crash, have to try to organise themselves and survive, without the benefit of adult knowledge and expertise. They struggle to understand what has happened and endeavour to devise rules and rituals to cope with a situation in which anarchy could prevail. A member of the group becomes a victim of the dynamics and is killed for questioning a belief system which appeared to prevail.

A weakness of self-directed and student assessed counselling training can be a lack of teaching input from experienced supervisors on the grounds that they may become powerful or overbearing. This can lead to group dynamics becoming saturated by primitive feelings of competition and envy and subject to the prevailing prejudices and resistances of the group. As a result the group may be unchallenged by perspectives which promote competence as a counsellor. It has also been the case that some analytical training programmes have been slow to adopt a more transparent stance of assessing supervisees' capacity to learn, so that a formal trainee self-assessment becomes a factor, along with supervisors' reports, in evaluating competence.

A discussion which polarises the position of 'teacher' and 'pupil' is overpreoccupied with the respective roles, but fails to emphasise the actual process of learning, as a more neutral and mutual activity. In this sense it may be more fruitful to consider supervision as a space for learning in which a supervisee has the opportunity to develop professionally in the presence of a supervisor who is also open to stimulation and challenge. At times the supervisor may have to manage high levels of anxiety and tread the fine line between the polarities of overactive interference in the process of the therapy being supervised, and a permissive stance which fails to challenge.

Supervisees who are 'spoon fed' may fail to thrive as much as those who are left to forage for themselves.

Clinical discussion

In the example given the supervisor attempted to draw some comment from the supervisee but she quickly got drawn into making her own comments and then provided some reading material. She seemed to get drawn into a more didactic mode of interaction which the supervisee hears as instruction but fails to internalise this as a comment on the process of the therapy. He subsequently draws attention to the patient's inability to play with him which seems to reflect his need rather than that of the patient, i.e., 'I need you to play with me'. The patient is not allowed the space to discover how to play. It seems as if the supervisee was not sufficiently able to understand the nature of the patient's resistance which contributed towards the ending of the therapy. This raises issues about the supervisor's capacity to explore the dynamics that were 'at play' in the supervision.

Brain development as the basis for learning

The foundations of a basic capacity to 'learn' are laid in infancy and provide the platform for the building of more formal educative processes. Both parties in the supervisory relationship will have had a long history of learning experience in a variety of educational institutions and vocational settings. If we can comprehend something of the formative aspects of mental functioning in infancy then some light may be thrown on the operation of adult minds. It is then relevant to ask the question, 'What are the basic components of the learning process, how do the components develop and what can input about mental functioning contribute to our understanding of the way learning takes place in supervision?'

Contemporary research into the development of the brain's capacity to absorb and process information is based on studies of the working brain of neonates through the use of brain scans, electrodes attached to the scalp to monitor the transmission of electrical impulses, and the inputting of data into computer models of the brain. Patterns of brain functioning can be correlated with observed stimuli from the external environment.

The American researcher Bruce D. Perry (Perry et al., 1995) contributes to our understanding of the way the central nervous system develops and of maladaptive reactions that may impair learning.

A detailed description of brain functioning is beyond the scope of this chapter and the limits of the author's understanding. A number of general points which relate brain function to patterns of learning will hopefully add to the discussion.

Perry argues that in order for the brain to develop it must be subject to stimulation. He defines this as 'use-dependent neurological change'. The brain is constructed of approximately one hundred million brain cells or neurones, each of which has a capacity to absorb stimuli that impact upon it and to transmit the energy to adjacent cells through a chemical reaction. The sources of stimuli are either the external environment through touch, sight, smell and hearing or from internal mental processes such as memory or emotions. The brain is subject to a continual cascade of input, and under usual conditions, this promotes a state of pulsating neuronal activity of reactive excitation or output. The natural plasticity of the brain is such that neurones respond to stimulation but revert to their original state. If however, patterns are of sufficient intensity and frequency, a pathway evolves that predisposes a series of neurones to a pattern of receptivity. These occur in local networks, and with increased levels of exposure and complexity of response, lead to neural pathways that link different areas of the brain.

In the course of normal maturation the brain develops in a sequential manner from the neonate's early primitive brain stem activity governing heartbeat and breathing, to the complex cognitive and multi-functional activity of later life. Hormonal triggers play a part in brain development but the receptivity of brain functioning to these is dependent on developmental stimulation. The essential point is that if the brain is not used it will fail to develop its inherent potential and that repeated experience creates templates through which all new experience is filtered. 'The more a neural network is activated, the more there will be use-dependant internalisation of new information needed to promote survival' (Perry et al., 1995: 275).

Learning in that sense is a physical event. Tresan (1996), writing from a Jungian perspective, refers to this process as instantiation – learning registering 'in the flesh'. He links this to the inherited developmental structure of the brain and the predisposition to seek a response from the environment or, to use the Jungian frame of reference, the archetypal need of the self to seek experience in order to realise the potential for growth.

We adapt to our environs or perish – biologically we 'learn' to survive. Such adaptation involves not only the acquisition of basic motor skills and social interaction, but also the capacity to react to stress and manage consequent anxiety. Perry observes that the effect of repeated exposure to undue stress or trauma stimulates over-development of specific mental pathways to the extent that internal reaction becomes disproportionate to the level of sensory input. He discusses the primitive fight/flight response which is active in neonate brain activity as an arousal response, or in the case of exposure to trauma, hyper-arousal. To this he adds the freeze response which in effect shuts down the central nervous system, blocking out any input from external stimuli. He defines this over exposure to stress as sensitisation, summing this up in the phrase 'states become traits'.

Given that the focus of this chapter is the process of learning in the supervisory setting, the disruption caused by under-stimulation and by trauma is of some interest. Clearly many of the patients brought by supervisees will have had major disruptions in the development of their mental capacity. We must also be mindful of areas in which a supervisee, and for that matter the supervisor, may be 'sensitised' and prone to hyper-arousal in anxiety-provking situations.

The observation that learning is a process that physically alters the brain by promoting the development of mental pathways through the frequency and intensity of stimuli, accords with Szecsödy's (1990) notion that learning is a mutative experience.

Mental development and the role of a care-giver

Perry draws attention to the effect of experience on brain structure. This leaves open to question the nature of the experience to which we are subjected. Alan

Schore (1996) draws attention to ways in which the structure of our mental functioning is influenced by the impact of external stimulation. He specifically refers to the impact of care-givers on neonates.

Schore summarises research by himself and others, which is helpful in our attempts to understand the process of learning by advancing Bowlby's (1969) thinking about attachment behaviour. Schore starts from the principle that the brain is a self-organising system and that self-regulation is a fundamental principle of human life. He indicates that the part of the brain located in the right hemisphere is designed to manage affect regulation and arousal regulation. This function is active from the first weeks of life.

The brain's self-organising capacity develops within the context of a relationship with another self, another brain. Close contact with a care-giver is essential for the internal biochemical regulation of the infant's early mental functioning as this maintains a context in which there is a balanced rhythm between moments of arousal and rest, day and night. This is as important as vigilance over temperature regulation and fluid intake. The care-giver's presence manages the intensity and duration of experience and attempts to regulate a balanced and holding environment. A well managed physical and emotional setting is defined as a state of *co-regulation*. As the infant develops skills of locomotion and language, a sense of personal agency and a concept of self or identity, the capacity to self regulate steadily increases. Care-givers serve to function as a reference point to which the child can retreat to co-regulate and recover.

Bion (1962/1984) developed the idea of maternal reverie in which he advanced the notion of the mother containing the baby through a deep capacity to think and that such activity is the basis from which the baby will begin to develop his own capacity for thought. In terms of the discussion such reverie is active and 'co-regulating' in effect.

Winnicott (1960) called such deep thought 'maternal preoccupation'. Winnicott's focus is wider than Bion's and he considers the mother/baby unit as part of the holding environment which provides the basis for the infant's development.

Schore (1996) argues that inconsistent or unreliable care disrupts the infant's basic rhythm of life and may promote a reversion to a state of premature self regulation in a desperate attempt to maintain its equilibrium. Individuals who have been subjected to inconsistent co-regulation develop patterns of insecure attachment or an inappropriate tendency to *self regulate*. The capacity to take in, retain and utilise information may also be affected.

Langs (1994) takes the notion of disruption and applies this to the effect of unhelpful interventions in the therapeutic setting. He argues that patients who experience their therapist as acting carelessly in relation to the therapeutic frame will obliquely convey their feelings to the therapist. Such cues may be conscious and unconscious and through action as well as word. If the therapist picks up these 'encoded messages', acknowledges the distress and adjusts his behaviour, the patient will respond with signs of approval or encoded validations.

The therapist aims to provide and promote a capacity to think in their work with the patient and it is also important that the supervisor builds reverie with the supervisee. One of the functions of the supervisor is to provide a holding environment in which the supervisee is able to think about the patient and recover their personal equilibrium in the face of the impact of the patient's distress and the weight of the projections to which they are subjected. An aspect of the recovery of the capacity to think is an awareness of the effects of breaks in the therapeutic framework. In other words the supervisor helps co-regulate the supervisee's mental functioning just as they, in turn, holds the patient. The supervisee is therefore enabled to think about, and learn from, the experience.

Clinical discussion

In the case under discussion the supervisor attempted to provide some space for thinking but then got drawn into 'pushing the pace' by introducing theoretical material which the supervisee was not ready to consider. The supervisee then attempted to inappropriately manage the patient so that the levels of anxiety escalated in both the patient and the supervisee.

The clinical example raises the question as to the extent to which the supervisee felt contained or held in mind by the supervisor so as to enable recovery from the impact of the patient and recovery of the capacity to think.

Scanning sensory input to learn the 'grammar' of experience

Research quoted in *The Guardian* (Radford, 1998) indicates that from a young age infants respond to the sound of language. By four and a half months they are able to understand the grammatical structure of language. Scientists invented an entirely new nonsense language to which the infants were exposed and by eight months they had learnt to parse it and segment it into words. It was not until they were 18 months old that they began to understand what words meant and subsequently to build up a vocabulary. It seems likely that infants scan the influx of sensory data in a way which is global and unfocused – each moment is experienced for what it is until the use of language begins to structure their mental life in a new way.

The *Guardian* article could provide a basic metaphor for the process of early learning namely, infants scan their environment in an attempt to understand the underlying patterns or the 'grammar' of experience. It would seem that such scanning is constant and often subliminal in nature. In the course of maturation the infant is able to build on the underlying patterns and discover meaning, language and identity. This enables them to develop their own dialogue with their environs, to interact with others and ultimately as an adult to be a successful care-giver themselves. Adults are not subjected to the same pressure to master new experience as infants but they retain a capacity to monitor experience and to scan their environment for indicators that may lead to benign or threatening situations.

The image of infants scanning the environment to structure the rhythm and shape of their experience is a helpful one. Searles (1975) writes of the role reversal in which the patient unconsciously acts as 'therapist to their analyst.' When applied to the supervisory setting there is a sense in which part of the supervisee's attention is focused, often unconsciously, on being 'supervisor to the supervisor'. The 'observing ego' plays a part in the therapeutic alliance in both therapy and supervision.

Casement (1985) drew attention to the supervisee's development of the 'internal supervisor'. This refers to the capacity to monitor one's own work from a more detached internal position from which one can make trial identifications. That is, the supervisee can develop the capacity to think about the impact of their interventions on the patient in a way which internalises the role of supervisor.

Clinical discussion

It is open to question to what extent the patient was looking for clues in the manner of the therapist's response to her request for homework. Was the therapist able to reflect on the meaning of the request for homework or the complaint that he was too intrusive in what he was saying to the patient about play? Could he note his own irritation and and think about this in relation to the patient?

The supervisee was probably looking for indications of the supervior's reaction to the material. Some supervisees will easily pick up positive responses while others may be much more sensitised towards negative feedback. In the case under discussion the supervisor did not seem sufficiently alive to signs of anxiety in the supervisee.

Memory

Memory is a central component to the process of learning. Without this there can be no accumulation or continuity of experience. Perry et al. (1995) concludes that there is no discrete area of brain function which is a specific repository of memory. The activity of remembering entails a complex putting together of information from various areas of brain functioning. Sophisticated tasks such as playing the piano or, for that matter the activity of supervision, require a complex remembering that draws on many systems within the brain. These include, among others, cognition and the ability to reconstruct our perception of an event. We can hold about seven items in active memory, but many thousands more in a state accessible to recall. Because individuals have different accumulated experience, different paths of neural development and different states of arousal, they will register any given event in an idiosyncratic manner. What they perceive and what they are able to recall from memory will have its own bias.

Memory and the supervisory process

Supervisees report on their work to their supervisors. Such reporting is subject to the supervisee's own perceptual distortion and dependent on the supervisee's memory of what happened. If reporting is done on the basis of notes written after the session, then supervisor and supervisee are at least in part sharing in a fantasy of what happened. Even if full audio or video recordings were available the emotional affect, as experienced by the supervisee, will be absent unless it is reported separately.

The concept of memory extends wider than that of factual discourse. Given what has been said about sensitisation and hyper-arousal, it is likely that the supervisee will recall both the perceived emotional response of the patient and their reactions at a feeling level, at given points in a therapy session. The evocation of either emotional pain or a dysfunctional response may be one of the most informative contributions to the learning process in supervision. A supervisee may become tearful, be unable to remember what happened and apparently lose the capacity to think. It is of fundamental importance to treat unconscious processes with respect so that the impact of anxiety on the ability to recall is taken into account. When supervisors listen to a supervisee's account they are not dealing with an objective event, but a remembered interpretation of what occurred, twice removed. What is forgotten may be as important as what is remembered.

Internal processes and defences against anxiety

When individuals are placed in situations in which levels of stress and anxiety threaten their sense of personal equilibrium, they will very often revert to more infantile survival techniques.

From her experience of working with small children, Melanie Klein (1975) noted the formation of primitive emotional defences as a means of coping with the bewildering impact of experience and the anxiety which this provokes. Adult care-givers seemed to be regarded as either the source from which good experience is dispersed and taken in or a depository into which all unwanted feelings are offloaded. She defined this as the paranoid-schizoid position.

Klein argued that a significant milestone in emotional development occurs along with the realisation that a care-giver can be good and bad and therefore loved and hated at the same time. It is a painful realisation that the loved person may also be subjected to destructive impulses and out of this conflict emerges the ability to make reparation and tolerate a sense of guilt. Klein defined this as the depressive position. Klein argues that the ability to move from primitive reactive defences to the proactive functioning of the depressive position is a crucial component of emotional development. Under duress adults may revert to paranoid-schizoid levels of functioning and the capacity to recover to the depressive position is a feature of adult mental health.

The learning position

Martinez del Pozo (1997) develops the concept of the *learning position*. The learning position, like that of the depressive position, is essentially one in which the learner is sufficiently mature to cope with ambivalent feelings exposed by uncertainty.

Learning exposes the individual to stimuli, which perplex, excite or frighten. It is a painful aspect of learning to have one's omnipotence and well formulated patterns of thinking thrown open to question, and the subsequent feelings of anger and discomfort evoked can be disturbing.

The participants in the supervisory setting are not exempt from this exposure and under the sway of excessive anxiety can revert to primitive and defensive ways of thinking. The capacity to learn oscillates between retreat to the paranoid-schizoid position and recovery to the depressive or learning position. She also postulates an intermediate position – the sensorial.

In a defensive frame of mind the supervisee may resort to splitting important figures into rigid categories of good and bad. They may split between different supervisors, between supervisor and personal therapist, between the supervisor and the administration or between fellow supervisees and the organisation. The supervisee may idealise a supervisor and, while this may be initially helpful, if it persists learning will be inhibited. On the other hand the supervisee may denigrate a supervisor and treat them with open contempt or covert dismissal – a resistance to learning.

I find it difficult to understand what del Pozo means by the 'intermediate' or 'sensorial' position. I wonder if Steiner's formulation of 'psychic retreat' may be utilised to explore the intermediate position further. Psychic retreat is defined as a retreat from the conflict of the depressive position but also as an avoidance of the active and projective defence mechanisms of the paranoid-schizoid position. Essentially it is a state of psychological withdrawal activated as a defence mechanism. This can be either a defence against the strength of the projections to which the 'learner' is subjected or a defence against the supervisee's own aggression and unconscious wish to retaliate. The supervisee may become unable to think or to be available for their patient, they may become excessively self absorbed and unable to accept the input from supervision. At an extreme they may even fall victim to physical symptoms as a somatic manifestation of their anxiety. The unconscious aim of such a state is to survive and hold them together.

Supervisees who are inexperienced or are subject to heavy projections from their patient, may revert to paranoid-schizoid modes of functioning or retreat into withdrawal. The supervisor can provide a cathartic holding experience, a space to think, or in Schore's (1996) terminology the opportunity to co-regulate or recover to a more mature mode of functioning.

I would suggest that the concept of the learning position may be enhanced by consideration of the more neurotic conflicts implicit in the Oedipus complex. While the patient may be unaware of the supervisor, the supervisor-supervisee relationship is aware of the importance of the third party, the patient. In considering the dynamics of the supervisory relationship the move from the two person to three person relating should be kept in mind. The focus on learning difficulties will shift from the primitive envy and love/hate splitting of the paranoid-schizoid defences, through the battlefield of the struggle for autonomy and control, to the minefield of competition, rivalry and jealousy of fully developed Oedipal conflict. Such anxieties are often stirred up by the triangular constellation of supervisory material. The themes of inclusion and exclusion are prominent as is the struggle to move from a position of rivalry to that of finding role models with which one can identify and from whom a developing sense of identity can be incorporated.

Clinical discussion

The example which I gave demonstrated some clear indications of reversion to paranoid-schizoid modes of thinking. The supervisee appears to idealise the supervisor as a person of great experience. He also attempts to split between the supervisor and the clinical serivice. There may even be elements of contempt both for the patient who is not able to play and for the supervisor in the way the input is not understood.

Defences against learning in the training setting

My experience in a training institution has lead me to observe that many trainee psychodynamic counsellors go through an initial stage of training in which learning is beset by anxiety. This may lead to paranoid-schizoid, depressive and withdrawal defences. Operating in the therapeutic space in which they are required to be both participant and observer is a new and stressful enough experience, without having the additional anxiety of reporting to a supervisor. The reversion to defensive positions is endemic in the training situation, but what is of paramount importance is the ability to recover and reflect, in other words to learn. One of the satisfactions of working with trainees is observing the gathering pace of learning and professional competence.

The staff on the course that provides training in supervision at the WPF Counselling and Psychotherapy, have noted that trainee supervisors undergo a very similar process. Very experienced psychotherapists or counsellors often find themselves in a position of confusion and discomfort as they grapple with acquiring a new skill, that of holding a supervisee and patient in mind. Areas of difficulty or personal blockages that may have been previously untouched are stirred up, temporarily activating the more paranoid-schizoid defences against learning. The underlying Oedipal nature of the triangular configuration of the task can also 'ambush' trainees from oblique and unexpected angles.

Organisational pressures and the learning process

It is necessary to note in passing the supervisor's obligation to bear in mind the effects of organisational pressure on the learning environment. Ekstein and Wallerstein (1958), through the concept of the clinical rhombus remind us of the powerful effect of the administrator on the supervisory process. Szecsödy (1997) and del Pozo (1997) expand on this. In holding the boundaries of the process, the supervisor will have to make judgements as to how he contains organisational pressures in order to protect the learning experience of the supervisee.

Finding what is there to be learned – assimilative and accommodative learning

Earlier in the chapter (p. 71) I drew attention to Szecsödy's (1990) reference to learning as a mutative experience. Szecsödy draws attention to Piaget's (1958) distinction between assimilative and accommodative learning. Assimilative learning refers to the ability to take in information, adding to the 'data base' which is already established. Accommodative learning refers to 'encounters with new information [that] result in a fundamental modification of existing cognitive schemata, so that the new encounter can be dealt with' (Szecsödy, 1997: 109). In Perry's terms a 'use-dependent' change in mental functioning has been stimulated. Learning, in this sense, promotes change and development.

Szecsödy links Piaget's categories of learning to Ekstein and Wallerstein's (1958) notion of 'dumb spots' and 'blind spots' in the understanding of a supervisee. The terminology is dated but the underlying concepts are helpful. 'Blind spots' refer to a lack of basic information whereas 'dumb spots' refer to a lack of understanding. Their observations led to the conclusion that supervisors too often confused the two states, supplying additional information on theory or technique rather than addressing the supervisee's inability to understand or process the dynamics they were presenting. In other words they were confusing assimilative with accommodative learning. Additional information increased the level of anxiety in the supervisee.

I also referred earlier in the chapter (p. 72) to Winnicott's notion of the holding environment provided by the supervisor. At this point I want to make reference to the way he extends the use of the concept of the transitional object to the realm of cultural experience (Winnicott, 1971). Much of our cultural heritage in terms of music, art or literature exists already but it is also there to be found. If it is not taken, utilised and internalised it remains as a potential rather than a living entity. The literature relating to psychoanalytical or psychodynamic therapy exists too, but it has to be 'found' and internalised. Part of the educative process of supervision is helping the supervisee to 'find' or assimilate the theory but to go further and to accommodate or internalise this as part of their way of being with patients. It is therefore, of particular importance to link this to the idea of discriminating between so called 'blind' and 'dumb' spots which inhibit learning in the supervisee. It is also necessary to develop insight into the individual learning patterns of supervisees if we are to facilitate genuine learning. I turn to this in my final section.

Clinical discussion

The supervisor seemed unable to stay with the supervisee's difficulty and got drawn into providing 'assimilative' information in the face of the anxiety expressed by their supervisee. The patient too, seems to be very anxious. It may have been more helpful to have stayed with the difficulty around resistance shown by the patient and to have thought about the blocks in the therapy and the counter-transference feelings in the supervisee.

Individual styles of learning

Carl Jung in his discussion of the theory of types (Jung, 1931) reminds us that individuals vary in their inherent disposition. As a result the differing mental functions of thinking, sensation, intuition and feeling may predominate in one individual as opposed to another. The observations of Perry et al. (1995) and Schore (1996) draw attention to the way in which inherited potential is affected by the experience. The variation in experience from one person to another leads to the employment of differing defensive mechanisms. People may also have varied educational experiences and learning histories. It follows that supervisors need to take into account that supervisees will have different cognitive styles and will learn in different ways as a consequence of these experiences.

Jacobs et al. (1995) list four modes of thought that operate in supervisees: the inductive, the associative, the creative and the self-reflective. These modes of thought are utilised by all supervisees but will predominate more in one supervisee than in another. Because the initial reaction to the material differs, the point of entry into thinking about the material will vary. It is important to utilise areas of greater strength as a starting point to learning, but also to be mindful of areas of mental functioning which need to be developed in the complex process of becoming a therapist.

Inductive thinking

Supervisees with a strongly developed sense of logic will have competence in inductive thinking. They will draw inferences from particular experiences in order to make at least a tentative attempt to link this with general principles. The hypotheses which follow can be changed and reformulated, and they are at best a compass bearing in a sea of uncertainty enabling orientation towards a point of reference. The supervisor should attempt to safeguard against rigidity of thought, which imposes rather than infers understanding, both in the supervisee and themselves.

Associative thinking

Other supervisees may be more adept at noting random thoughts, spontaneous images or daydreams, which the material provokes. These can occur either in the process of the therapy or when thinking retrospectively. Associative thinking is defined as joining one thought to another without an immediate conscious goal – x leads me to think about y. Such thoughts are intuitive, random and occur with little initial understanding of process.

Freud encouraged his patients to free associate but supervisees and supervisors can also use the technique. As in all supervisory interactions it is vital that the therapeutic endeavour of working with the patient remains in focus, lest associations drift into the realms of private fantasy. The patient's associations are a primary source of information, those of the supervisee may provide access to the counter-transference, and the supervisor's associations may also be an informative source of understanding. A supervisor's task is to encourage the supervisees to develop a capacity to associate, so that they can learn to suspend logic and allow the unconscious to 'speak'. I think that supervisors should give voice to their associations sparingly, lest they dilute the impact of the supervisees' presentation and inhibit their development.

Creative thinking

Creative thinking is linked to the capacity to play, to use the material at hand and to build upon it. Supervisor and supervisee conduct their relationship on the basis of the supervisee's reported interaction with the patient, which is subject to the inadequacy of memory and distortions of perception to which we all are prone. The patient's story too, is a similar mixture of fact and fantasy and their impact on the inner world.

What is reported in supervision is an approximation of what occurred in the session with the patient, linked to the thoughts, feelings and emotions present in the supervisee. Supervisor and supervisee play with the material and reconstruct in their imaginations the interaction that is being reported. Learning through play is an important part of the supervisory experience but caution is needed least the focus on the patient is lost in the sense of excitement about possible meanings in the material.

Self-reflective thinking

Self-reflective thinking causes the mind to reflect on itself in terms of the thoughts, feelings, memories and sensations which excite the activity of the brain. But it is also able to reflect on the overall sense of agency – who am I, why am I doing this and what am I doing right now? Supervisees are subject to a bewildering array of stimuli which constitute the raw material of the data to be processed. They have to learn to make sense of such material, in order to organise and retain it. Supervisees' difficulties in processing and prioritising their thoughts about supervision must be recognised, so that blockages and resistances to learning can be worked on. It is also important that a supervisee is encouraged to reflect on their strengths as well as their weaknesses. Self-reflection however, has to remain linked to the task in hand, so that work with the patient is not lost in a cloud of self absorbed thinking.

The supervisor is then aiming to facilitate the development of various modes of thinking in the supervisee. The aim is to use those modes of thinking which are prevalent in the supervisee and to encourage other modes of thought which may be less developed. In short, to build upon strengths, but also to encourage the growth of under-developed ways of thinking.

Clinical discussion

The supervisee in the example given is able to allow the material to impact upon him in a way that produced a dream. It is open to question to what extent he was able to use the associative thinking to link this with the patient material. It is not clear if the dream refers to his own resistance, if so his capacity for self-reflection seems under-developed. He also appears to be unable to understand the nature of play and to have difficulty in using his capacity for logical thought to begin to think about relevant clinical concepts.

It would seem the most obvious course of action for the supervisor would be to work with the supervisee's capacity to think intuitively.

In the material given the supervisor seems to demonstrate that her strongest area of functioning lies in the inductive mode. She also attempts to work at the creative mode of functioning, though this seems to be more cerebral than actually playful. Not enough thought seemed to be given to how the personal style of supervisor and supervisee inter-relate.

Conclusion

I have in the course of this chapter looked at the interface between teaching and supervision and examined the ways in which supervisors can promote learning in the supervisory setting without becoming too much the teacher. In order to survive we have to adapt to our environment or, in other words, to learn. Our early experience is of critical importance. Good enough experience and favourable neuro-biological development leads to a reasonable capacity to learn. We learn to hold things in mind through our having experience of being held in mind so that our emotional affect is regulated within a tolerable range of intensity.

The supervisor then, functions as the 'third eye' who sees things from a different perspective and, as such, can ensure that the patient has an advocate if the supervisee fails to hear or understand them. It is not the supervisor's role 'to know' but to facilitate understanding in the supervisee. The supervisor is a container who enables the supervisee to think and to cope with the primitive defences against anxiety and to recover to the learning position. Understanding the unique manner in which each supervisee functions in the face of the vicissitudes of experience and by dint of personal predisposition is an important part of the supervisory function.

As Casement (1985) reminds us, a vital component in developing understanding is learning from the patient, who teaches the supervisor and supervisee much of what they need to know in order to understand what it is that so pains them.

References

Bion, W. (1962/1984) *Learning from Experience*. London: Karnac Books.

Bowlby, J. (1969) *Attachment and Loss*. London: Hogarth Press.

Casement, P. (1985) *On Learning from the Patient*. London: Tavistock Publications.

del Pozo, M. (1997) 'On the process of supervision in psychoanalytic psychotherapy', in B. Martindale (ed.), *Supervision and its Vicissitudes*. London: Karnac Books. pp. 39–59.

Dickens, C. (1854/1964) *Hard Times*. New York: The New American Library of World Literature.

Ekstein R., and Wallerstein R., (1958) *The Teaching and Learning of Psychotherapy*. New York: Basic Books.

Gitterman, A. (1977) 'Comparison of Educational Models and their Influences on Supervision' in F.W. Kaslow (ed.) *Supervision, Consultation and Staff Training in the Helping Professions*. San Francisco, CA: Jossey Bass.

Golding, W. (1954) *Lord of the Flies*. New York: Perigee.

Jacobs D., David, P. and Meyer, D. (1995) *The Supervisory Encounter*. New Haven, CT and London: Yale University Press.

Jung, C. (1931) *A General Description of Types*, Collected Works, 16. London: Routledge.

Klein, M. (1975) *The Collected Works of Melanie Klein*. London: Hogarth Press.

Langs, R. (1994) *Doing Supervision and Being Supervised*. London: Karnac Books.

Mattinson, J. (1975/1992) *The Reflection Process in Case Work Supervision*. London: Tavistock Institute.

Perry, D., Pollard, R., Blakely, T., Baker, W. and Vigilante, D. (1995) 'Childhood Trauma, the Neurobiology of Adaptation, and "Use-dependent" Development of the Brain: How "States" Become "Traits"', *Infant Mental Health Journal*, 16(4): 271–91.

Piaget, J. (1958) *The Development of Thought: Equilibration of Cognitive Structures*. New York: Viking.

Radford, T. (1998) 'Babies are good at grammar, scientists decide' *The Guardian*, 17 February.

Schore, A. (1996) 'The experience dependent maturation of a regulatory system in the orbital prefrontal cortex and the origin of developmental psychopathology', *Development and Psychopathology* 8 (1996): 59–87.

Searles, H. (1975) 'The Patient as Therapist to his Analyst' in P.L. Giovacchini (ed.) *Tactics and Techniques in Psychoanalytic Therapy, Volume II: Countertransference*. New York: Jason Aronson. pp. 95–151.

Stimmel, B. (1995) 'Resistance to awareness of the supervisor's transferences with special reference to the parallel process', *The International Journal of Psycho-Analysis* 76(6): 609–618.

Szecsödy, I. (1990) 'Supervision: a didactic or mutative situation', *Psychoanalytic Psychotherapy*, 4(3): 245–361.

Szecsödy, I. (1997) '(How) is learning possible in supervision?', In B. Martindale (ed.), *Supervision and its Vicissitudes*. London: Karnac Books. pp. 101–116.

Tresan, D. (1996) 'Jungian metapsychology and neurobiological theory', *The Journal of Analytical Psychology*, 41(3): 399–436.

Winnicott, D. (1960) *The Theory of the Parent-Infant Relationship* London: Hogarth Press.

Winnicott D. (1971) 'The location of cultural experience', in D. Winnicott *Playing and Reality* London: Tavistock Publications. pp. 95–103.

PART III

THE SETTING AND SUPERVISION

Chapter 6

The Geography and Topography of Supervision in a Group Setting

Christine Driver

Group supervision of one-to-one work was introduced by many counselling and therapeutic agencies as an economic and efficient way of providing supervision. But what is the nature of the beast that was created? In Langs's terms (1994) group supervision of one-to-one work is a frame deviation in that the supervision frame does not match or mirror the therapeutic frame. On the other hand group supervision provides a depth and breadth of resources which one-to-one supervision does not. Group supervision immediately confronts the supervisor with a need to hold at least two different modes of operation (i.e., supervision and group process) and at least three frames of reference (i.e., the needs of the individual (supervisee and client), the needs of the group and the needs of the organisational frame in which the supervision group is set). The challenge to the supervisor therefore is to enable the group to work and function as a supervision group in which the dynamics of the work can be mirrored and processed, and the dynamics of the group contained and managed.

Supervision as a process depends on the way in which the supervisor balances the basic modes of supervisory activity. This activity combines the functions of containment (holding), processing, structuring and the development of a questioning attitude and observing ego within the supervisee. It is this activity within the context of group supervision that I want to explore in more depth. This chapter will therefore look at how good clinical practice and counsellor/therapist development can be facilitated through the experience and dynamics of group supervision. In addition it will consider the importance and significance of the interactional elements within the group, the group process and group environment and the problems that can develop from this.

The geography of the group and group context

A supervision group, whether it is in an agency, a training organisation or the NHS etc., operates within a context which has its own external agendas. These external agendas are important because they define the geography in which the group is set and the elements of the interactional matrix. For example a group which has been set up to provide supervision for beginner counsellors within the context of a training organisation has an immediately defined supervisory task and external agendas. These tasks and agendas will involve the supervisor in processes of assessment and training and may involve them working in a style that is congruent with the demands and orientation of the training organisation. A different set of external agendas will revolve around a supervision group set up in an NHS setting. Here the amount of therapy offered may be time limited and defined, to some extent, by funding and these elements will determine the supervisory task of the group. Whatever the setting, the external tasks and agendas, whether explicit or implicit, will determine and affect the supervisory task of the group.

Internally, however, the supervision group has its own geography which comprises the aspirations, hopes, needs and problems of the individuals within the group and these will inevitably affect how the group operates in practice. The supervisor is therefore gathering up and holding information at many different levels. At a primary level there is a gathering up of the client material and the clinical issues involved. Overlapping this are the issues of the supervisees and the manifestations of their internal world plus the issues of the agency and its internal agendas. The geography and topography of the group therefore comprises many different aspects which reflect the elements of the clinical rhombus and the interactive field in which the supervision group is operating.

Bion comments that a 'work group is constantly perturbed by influences which come from other group mental phenomena' (Bion 1989: 129), and certainly a supervision group is an example of this. To this I would add, however, that a work group is affected by the mental phenomena within the clinical rhombus, for example, agency issues, management issues, supervisory issues and personal issues all of which affect the supervisory task but may, if held and understood, enhance the supervisory process. The challenge for the supervisor is how to hold and work with the various expressions of group phenomena within the structure and function of a group whose task is supervision. Externally the setting of the supervision group and the contract will determine the field in which the group operates. Internally the way the supervision group functions and what it focuses on will be influenced by the supervisory attitude of the supervisor and the supervisees. The supervisory attitude needs to mirror a focus on 'the work', i.e., the development of the clinical work by the supervisee, and it is this that reflects the underlying agenda of the group. However, the group dynamics cannot be ignored. For the group to develop into an effective work group a level of trust and group cohesiveness (Yalom, 1995) must develop and the supervisor and supervisees need to manage the unconscious mechanisms and familial dynamics inherent in the group and the processes of supervision. Having said that, group supervision, far from being just an economic necessity, can provide a reflective and supportive milieu and become a rich and valuable tool in the development of clinical work, supervisee development and good clinical practice.

At a fundamental level consideration needs to be given to the parameters and frame of the supervision group in terms of the frequency of meetings and the number of supervisees per group, so that from the start it can be experienced as a safe container in which both the clinical work and the supervisee can develop. A supervision group consisting of, say, six or more supervisees and with a potentially unlimited number of clients will not be experienced as a safe container either for the supervisees or the supervisor. Such a situation will present an overwhelming demand on both the group and the supervisor and the work done will be little more than containment at best, and may add to anxiety and frustration rather than being a setting for exploration and processing. For the supervision group to function it needs to contain and manage, at a more or less optimal level, the needs of the clients and the needs of the supervisees. If the agency or supervisor cannot demand this then the group starts from an overburdened and potentially demoralised point. For the development of a working supervision group one needs a group environment that feels contained, where anxieties are not too overwhelming and where trust and intimacy can develop. If a group is too large, the number of clients held too great, or the anxieties within it too high it will be hard for it to function and the elements of acting out, splitting and projection will all too easily dominate.

A one-and-a-half hour weekly supervision group of four counsellors, containing a maximum of 12 clients and with two supervisees presenting each week is a workable framework for established clinicians. Allowing five to ten minutes at the beginning for any client issues needing immediate attention, and about five minutes at the end to reflect on any difficulties arising within the group process, either from the client presentations or the individual interactions, can also be containing. The tension that needs to be continually held is that the group is not a therapy group but a supervision group and, to quote Brookes, the supervisor has 'to embody a "symbolic attitude" which allows for an unfolding of psychological awareness within the group' (1995: 120). This symbolic supervisory attitude needs to maintain a focus on the clinical issues presented so as to enable the supervisee to develop their work with the client.

The supervision group

The nature, character and dynamics of a supervision group is determined by the personalities, personal pathologies (including the supervisor's), and the level of development of the individual members of the group. Irrespective of whether the supervisees are beginner counsellors/therapists or a mixture of experienced and inexperienced, the personal equation of each member will determine the character of the group. Kalsched comments that groups are 'breeding grounds for unconscious processes, including projection, splitting, acting out, to say nothing of dysfunctional family dynamics such as sibling rivalry, envy, scapegoating, triangulated collusive alliances, codependency etc.' (1995: 111). He goes on to cite Bion: 'every group is really two groups. The first is a work group, and the second, a basic assumption (the Ba-group), characterized by primitive unconscious fantasy dynamics, high levels of anxiety, and paranoid/schizoid splitting defenses' (1995: 111). There is, inevitably, a struggle between the function and needs of the supervision group (work group) and the needs of the individuals within it. It is this tension that makes group supervision a more complex task. The supervisor needs to understand the nature of group process and how unconscious anxieties manifest themselves in the group as well as the processes of supervision. Bion (1989) defines the acting out of anxieties within a group as basic assumption phenomena and he outlines them as dependency, fight/flight and pairing. All of these 'activities' within a group emerge as a consequence of the mental states and unconscious conflicts and issues of each individual member, and, within a supervision group, of the clinical material being presented. This, together with the issues of anxiety, envy, rivalry etc., are powerful factors for each member of the group and affect the group process and the way the group operates.

Of its very nature supervision is exposing, and potentially more so within a group context. Transference and projection onto the supervisor and other members of the group are inevitable and the degree and manner in which this occurs will determine the level of anxiety and unconscious enactments within the group, for example, pairing, resistance, retreats, aggression. Gertrud Mander in Chapter 10 reflects on the element of regression in supervision and this also needs to be taken into account. In most supervision groups there is a hierarchy, with the supervisor being the 'senior colleague'. The supervisee's internal response to this and the transference issues it generates will determine whether they are able to operate in the supervision group from a primarily 'adult' level or from an 'infantile' level. Unconscious identifications with the clinical material will also affect the way in which the supervisee presents and interacts in the group. The way in which these issues manifest themselves in the group will determine whether they are a resource or a hindrance to the supervisory process and will affect whether the group is functional or dysfunctional.

Supervision groups of beginner counsellors often exhibit basic assumption phenomena. Levels of anxiety and regression are often high and projections often place the supervisor into a fantasised omnipotent place. Frequently there is a polarisation between emptiness and fullness, a fantasy that as beginners they know nothing and that the supervisor knows it all. Sometimes the opposite may occur. An anxious supervisee may deny their anxiety by a bravado 'know it all' attitude. Either way projections and defences are in full swing as the beginner counsellor comes to experience uncertainty and anxiety in the face of the unknown and the dilemma of staying with the 'not knowing' and the process of discovery. Stoltenberg and Delworth comment that beginner or Level 1 trainees:

> tend to over accommodate to the supervisor, seeing this person as the all-knowing expert. In contrast, low awareness of others means that many supervisees at this level over assimilate with their clients, that is, they tend to view the client almost exclusively in terms of the supervisee's own previously developed cognitive structure. (1987: 52)

Thus beginner counsellors will tend to be dependent on the supervisor and be in processes of identification with the client. The task of the supervisor is to enable the supervisee to separate out from these identificatory patterns and to develop their own clinical identity with their own questioning and observing ego. The need to enable counsellor development, an observing ego, and a sense of self in relation to the client is perhaps most obvious with beginner counsellors.

A group of four beginner counsellors expressed their anxiety about starting work with clients through their initial questions of, 'How do we get our client into the room?' 'What do we say?' and 'How do we talk about contracts and fees?'. It became clear, both through their questions and their relationship to me, that they felt dependent on me and my 'knowledge'. Their sense of themselves as 'beginners' and their anxieties about this had instigated a defensive retreat into wanting to know 'the rules' and a demand on me as to 'how to do it'. In the following week one of the supervisees reported back on her first session and on what the client had said. When she had finished the group sat in silence and looked expectantly at me. There was a powerful expectation that I, as supervisor, would make some powerful and insightful comments on the client's psychopathology and the meaning of the client's communications. To have responded to these projections would, as Gee comments (Gee, 1996), have encouraged passivity and undermined their confidence and would have ignored one of the vital components of supervision, which is to enable the development of the supervisee. It was therefore important for me to try to tease out their thoughts, ideas and feelings so that the projection that I had all the 'valuable stuff' could be withdrawn. I needed to enable the supervisees to value their own ideas and to promote an integrative process that would enable the development of their own observing ego and internal supervisor. Instead of answering their questions I questioned them. What did they think the client was trying to tell them? What, in terms of the client's history, might determine the way the client related? What were their own feelings about the presented material and what did they think this might be telling them about the client? Through discussion and exploration the supervisees slowly became more confident in their own thoughts, ideas and feelings. They began to discuss their ideas more freely and to challenge each other and eventually challenge me. Sometimes their ideas did veer off into the extreme and I felt the need to take on a more navigational and structuring role but, by using a questioning and exploratory technique, there was a gradual withdrawal of the projections on to me and the group moved to being able to function as a work group with each supervisee being able to comment and think about each other's work.

As a supervisor of beginner counsellors one needs to understand how people learn and develop and John Stewart pursues this in Chapter 5. In addition the emotional needs of the supervisees, and how these affect the group, also need to be held and considered. In bringing these two points together, through the context of the clinical work, supervisee development can be promoted and the supervision group enabled to function as a work group. With new counsellors/therapists one needs to be thinking about what processes will enable them to develop their clinical skills and their work with individual clients. Szecsödy talks of how supervision should 'provide the trainee with the opportunity to reconstruct his interaction with the patient and to be able to reflect about the process and to increase his ability to use information' (1990: 250). He goes on to talk of the need for a learning alliance to enable a mutative learning situation and a supervisory attitude that is open, non-judgemental and non-competitive. Stoltenberg describes beginner 'trainees' as 'dependent on the supervisor: imitative, neurosis-bound, lacking self-awareness and other-awareness, categorical thinking with knowledge of theories and skills, but minimal experience' (1981: 60). Clearly these inner states are going to affect the processes of learning and development. The supervisor needs to aim to create an optimal environment in which the supervisee can develop their own internal capacity to deintegrate and integrate the information the client is bringing, and to be able to think about and process the symbolic, psychodynamic and emotional content of the material. The initial supervisory experience is critical for the setting up of an internal framework of thinking and processing within the supervisee. The supervisory process needs to mirror the internal processes of reflection, processing and reconstruction to enable the development of the supervisee's own 'internal supervisor' (Casement, 1985: 29).

Group supervision is a vital and valuable tool for this developmental process because a group provides a larger container for client/counsellor issues than one-to-one supervision. Supervisees can learn from each other and, facilitated by the supervisor, be encouraged to explore and play with ideas concerning the clinical material and the client/counsellor relationship. The focus in a group can move away from the potentially power loaded relationship of one-to-one supervision to a learning process which occurs through an interactive process with peers. Sproul-Boulton comments: 'a group can offer peer support. This is especially helpful for new or inexperienced staff who may view the whole process of supervision, with its connotations of criticism and possible humiliation, as fearful' (1995: 72). Being in a group means that diversity in terms of input of ideas and feelings cannot be ignored, all of which may reflect (or not) aspects of the client's struggles with their internal and external world. The group process and its facilitation by the supervisor therefore mirrors very effectively the internal mental processes which all counsellors/

therapists need to develop. Such a process involves a complex juggling of different pieces of information, thoughts, feelings, etc., which need to be integrated, processed and reconstructed to develop an understanding of the patient's world and the transference/counter-transference issues of the client/counsellor relationship.

For the supervisor the process of supervision within the group will also be affected by the states of identification between counsellor and client. The various basic assumption phenomena in the group and the unconscious identifications with the client's material will also trigger parallel processes. A particular example of this occurred in a group that consisted of four members, two men and two women of varying degrees of experience.

Keith was an experienced counsellor and Omid, the other male counsellor, had only been seeing clients for about six months. In one supervision session Omid presented a male client he had been seeing. During the presentation Keith continually interrupted Omid and became very animated as to how Omid should be working with his client. The two women in the group seemed excluded from this pairing and I became increasingly aware of Omid's passivity in relation to Keith's comments. This fight/flight pairing seemed to have become focused around issues of potency and power. I asked Omid what he felt about the way his client related to others. Omid commented that he felt the client often felt powerless and that it was hard for him to stand up for himself. I said I felt that this issue of power and powerlessness was being enacted in the group between Keith and Omid and perhaps reflected the nature of a split in the client with which Keith and Omid were variously identifying. My comment seemed to allow Keith and Omid to disengage from the fight and consider the powerful unconscious issues held within the client material which reflected the power/powerlessness split in his internal world and his external relationship. This split had become paralleled in the group by the unconscious identifications within Keith and Omid. This was highlighted by the fact that the group interaction had narrowed to these two members, while their differences in experience and confidence further highlighted the client's issues.

By using an awareness of basic assumption phenomena in the group and my reflections on my counter-transference, I was able to utilise another ingredient to develop an understanding of the client's internal world and the counsellor/client relationship. This insight enabled the supervisee and group members to reflect on what was happening to them and enabled them to use aspects of their own experience of the client to develop their understanding of the client's world and the client/counsellor relationship.

The two examples above illustrate in differing ways the effect of the supervisee's internal world on the functioning of the group and the processes within it. Sometimes these dynamics reflect the needs and issues of the supervisees and sometimes they reflect and parallel the dynamics of the client's internal world. What must also be borne in mind however is that the supervision group is not only affected by the internal world of the supervisees but also by that of the supervisor. The supervisor has to tolerate and reflect on their own counter-transference in relation to the clinical material presented and the supervisee presenting it. Processes of projection and projective-identification from the client will affect the group and the supervisor needs to separate these out from the supervisee; for example, a difficult and resistant client does not necessarily equal a difficult and resistant supervisee. However, the supervisor also needs to tolerate and reflect on their own transference and counter-transference in relation to the supervisee and the group. This may be especially true in a training situation where assessments are required and where transference and counter-transference may also inform the ongoing assessment of supervisee development. A supervisor can be informed of the ability of the supervisee not just by the evidence of their clinical work but also by their interaction with the supervisor and supervision group. For example, a quiet and deferential member of a supervision group was constantly experienced by the supervisor as dependent and needing narcissistic gratification that he was 'doing alright' with his clients. The supervisor's counter-transference helped her clarify her assessment of the supervisee as needing more time (and more therapy) to develop a stronger ego capacity to work with clients. Obviously this counter-transference observation could be made in one-to-one supervision but within a group setting the dynamics can be observed within the group interaction and they can help validate the counter-transference response. The use of the supervisor's counter-transference is however an area where the supervisor needs to be aware of their own 'blind spots' and transferences onto the supervisee. Barbara Stimmel comments:

> the supervision relationship is not simply organised around the clinical relationship between the supervisee and his patient; it is also susceptible to a 'sub-clinical' experience of transference in two directions ... [the] supervisor's unconscious transferences to the supervisee exist, and the parallel processes in a given supervision process lend themselves, among others, as likely contexts for the enactment of and resistance to the awareness of such transferences. (1995: 611)

In her paper Stimmel gives an example of how she realised she had taken on the role of a domineering mother to one of her supervisees which had led to the supervisee obeying her and remaining relatively passive. Resisting awareness of the supervisor's transferences onto supervisees within a group will inevitably cloud the group process and the supervisees will carry projections from the supervisor such as: the supervisor's favourite supervisee, the supervisee who becomes the scapegoat for the supervisor's negative projections, the supervisee that the supervisor feels needs a lot of 'feeding', etc. Supervisors therefore need to foster within themselves the same reflective and observing state that they are encouraging in their supervisees.

The ability of supervisors to reflect on their own transference and counter-transference responses allows a separation of the counter-transference responses which emanate from the reflection and parallel processes of the clinical material from the counter-transference responses in relation to the group members and the group norm and agenda, that emerge from their collective personalities and pathologies. The dilemmas relating to this were brought home to me when I was supervising a group where the group norm became very polarised and persistent.

A new supervision group, consisting of relatively experienced counsellors, remained consistently passive and withdrawn irrespective of the clinical material presented or attempts to explore the reflection and parallel processes. Following the presentation of clinical material by one of the supervisees, the other members would ask questions to clarify matters but rarely engaged in dialogue. I experienced a persistent and consistent group norm of defensive withdrawal, dependence and an overall lack of trust in a group supervisory alliance such that the group was barely able to function as a group let alone a supervision group. I found myself left with feelings of uselessness, fatigue and frustration. As I reflected to myself on my counter-transference and the passive withdrawal I experienced from the group members I reflected that, just as I was feeling angry at the group and doubtful about my ability to work, then perhaps the issue for all the supervisees was their doubt and anger about their abilities to work as counsellors. The level of depression, withdrawal and flight was, perhaps, because they doubted their abilities to be counsellors and hence, unconsciously, enviously attacked mine. As I began to formulate my counter-transference I could begin to think of how I needed to approach this within the process of supervision. It seemed to me that the unconscious anxiety of the supervisees, and perhaps the clients, was 'can we have hope in this process and can we trust that it is going to be nurturing?'. Until these fundamental issues could be mediated the group would continue to be dysfunctional. At around this time one of the supervisees brought a report of a session where the client wanted to finish the counselling abruptly. The supervisee thought this was a good idea but as we explored this her own doubts about the counselling process emerged. As we explored the psychodynamics of the client's material and why he might wish to 'fly off', the members of the group voiced their own anxieties about what they were able to offer clients. The group was then able to explore aspects of their own fantasies of what they had hoped they would achieve as counsellors and how they were struggling with reality and disillusionment, and finding that there weren't 'instant solutions'. This enabled the group norm to shift from its polarised and depressed place and move into a place where reality, frustration and uncertainty could be faced and struggled with.

This example illustrates the effect of the interplay of the various interactive levels within a supervision group. The group itself consisted of members of similar pathologies and personalities so that the group's response to anxiety and frustration created a group norm of passive withdrawal and frustrated rage. It was only when these anxieties and feelings could be understood and addressed through the clinical issues that the supervision group was able to function at a more optimal level.

The case also reflects the conflicts and limitations inherent within group supervision. A supervision group is, like any group, affected by the pathologies of the individuals within it. The interactive effect of this will determine whether the group will operate in a functional way, where creative intercourse can take place, or in a dysfunctional way as in the above example. The supervisor holds a very complex task in such a dysfunctional group. The supervisor has to walk a precarious tightrope between group conductor and supervisor while maintaining the focus on the work of supervision. The level of trust in any group will determine how far challenge and exploration can take place and this in turn will be determined by the levels of anxiety within the group. Anxiety, of varying degrees, is a factor in all supervision groups. It may encompass the wish for approval, fear of exposure or anxieties where the clinical material links to the supervisees' own unconscious material. How these anxieties are contained and handled will affect the attitude and development of the supervisee and the supervision group. However, anxiety may also be generated by the setting in which the supervision group operates.

The group environment and the interactive matrix

The interactive processes between group members and their unconscious identifications with aspects of the client material act as potential resources in the supervisory process. However, the supervision group is also contained within the frame of its environment and this can further influence what is brought to supervision. This complex interactive matrix contains client issues, group issues, supervisee issues, frame issues and issues relating to the field in which the supervision group is operating, which John Stewart explores further in Chapter 8. The framework and the field in which supervision operates are powerful factors which influence group process and as Langs comments: 'Throughout animate and inanimate nature, the frame or boundary conditions of an entity are a major determinant of the functioning and survival of that entity' (1994: 59). He goes on to add, 'In structuring a supervisory situation, it is essential to afford the systemic aspects and ground rules of the experience their full due' (1994: 59). The supervisor needs to be constantly aware of the dimensions of the interactive field and the way it influences the group agenda and the process of supervision. This became evident in a group I supervised within an agency which had a long waiting list and many clients presenting with painful and difficult histories, a number of them with HIV and bereavement-associated presenting problems.

A group of four supervisees started off in a cosy, friendly way and they were all very supportive of each other. Although this was very comfortable it began to leave me with the feeling that there was something difficult in relation to the work which we weren't reaching. A few weeks later one of the counsellors was absent and the clinical material presented revolved around issues of separation and of leaving relationships when disillusionment and disappointment set in. The discussion focused around anxieties about separation, loss and idealisation of mother/ other. The discussion however was 'sticky' and I felt it was hard for the group to challenge each other. I was also aware of the counsellor's absence and its effect. The following week this counsellor said she was going to leave the supervision group and the centre. The group was angry and anxious about this as they felt she was the senior counsellor and hence knew how to cope. There was anger at me too, that I was no longer the 'ideal' supervisor who could hold the group together. The clinical presentation that followed was of a client whom the counsellor described as being 'too much for me'. As we explored the 'demands' of the client and the counsellor's feelings about them, the feelings of the group also emerged. They felt the agency demanded too much and left them feeling they had to take on more clients. They expressed anxiety at working with so many very distressed and borderline clients and said they felt too much was expected of them. There was an overall group feeling of being overburdened and demoralised. I realised that I needed to take hold of this for the group so that the framework of the supervision group would feel safeguarded against too overt a pressure from the agency. The supervisees had come to feel unconscious victims of the agency's demands and were needing a supervisory 'parent' who could define and limit these demands so that they could feel contained, held and have their needs heard and understood. When their unconscious identification with the clinical material could be perceived and managed, the group was able to think and process more clearly the psychodynamics of the case.

Clarifying these unconscious identifications and holding onto the triangular nature of supervision within the interactive field encouraged a shift from shame, doubt, guilt and inferiority to autonomy, initiative and industry (Erikson, 1977). The shift enabled the development of the work and the development of the counsellor's therapeutic ego, which could think about and process the content of the client/counsellor interaction.

Conclusions

Group supervision provides an important and valuable forum for the supervisory process and the development of the supervisee. In spite of the difficulties it provides a resource which is absent in one-to-one supervision. Behr comments 'that a group which fosters open communication provides an antidote to isolation, and ... if this is true of therapeutic groups, it should be true of groups in which fellow therapists contemplate their work together' (1995: 17). It allows for a process of learning from each other in a place where ideas can be played with and transference and counter-transference explored and in which the supervisee can develop. All of these aspects of group supervision foster good clinical practice. Counsellors and therapists can all too easily become isolated and one-to-one supervision may foster an overvaluing of the supervisor's ideas against those of the supervisee. Group supervision provides an opportunity for members to explore issues together as well as mirror the internal conflicts and issues of the client. Overall therefore:

- Individuals in a supervision group are a resource of ideas and experience for each other.
- The sharing of thoughts, feelings and ideas within the supervisory process can mirror the internal mental processes which are needed to develop and evolve an 'observing ego' and an internal supervisor.
- Unconscious identifications by supervisees with the client's material and the subsequent reflection process and parallel process can open up the client's unconscious issues and aspects of the transference.
- Unconscious identifications with unworked areas of the supervisee's pathologies will affect the group process.
- The interactional matrix of the frame and setting of the group will affect the group agenda.
- Unconscious identifications within the interactional matrix will affect the supervision process and the group agenda.
- A mixture of personalities of supervisees is important to enable the group to function as a work group.
- The supervisor's internal reflection on their own counter-transference is vital to reflect on the concurrent processes within the group.

Group supervision was born out of necessity but it provides a rich and diverse container in which to explore, understand and develop clinical work and enable the development of the supervisees. It is a complex entity but because of this it provides a rich and active arena and an important forum for developing the supervisory process.

References

Behr, H.L. (1995) 'The Integration of Theory and Practice' in M. Sharpe (ed.) *The Third Eye. The Supervision of Analytic Groups*. London: Routledge. pp. 4–17.
Bion, W.R. (1989) *Experiences in Groups*. London: Routledge
Brookes, C.E. (1995) 'On Supervision in Jungian Continuous Case Seminars' in P. Kugler (ed.) *Jungian Perspectives on Clinical Supervision*. Einsiedeln, Switzerland: Daimon. pp. 119–127.
Casement, P. (1985) *On Learning from the Patient*. London: Tavistock Publications.
Erikson, E. (1977) *Childhood and Society*. London: Paladin.
Gee, H. (1996) 'Developing insight through supervision: relating, then defining', *The Journal of Analytical Psychology*, 41(4): 529–552.
Kalsched, D. (1995) 'Ecstasies and Agonies of Case Seminar Supervision' in P. Kugler (ed.) *Jungian Perspectives on Clinical Supervision*. Einsiedeln, Switzerland: Daimon. pp. 107–118.
Langs, R. (1994) *Doing Supervision and Being Supervised*. London: Karnac Books.
Sproul-Bolton, R. (1995) 'Supervision in the National Health Service. Part 1: Group Supervision in an Acute Psychiatric Unit' in M. Sharpe (ed.) *The Third Eye. The Supervision of Analytic Groups*. London: Routledge. pp. 71–76.

Stimmel, B. (1995) 'Resistance to awareness of the supervisor's transference with special reference to the parallel process', *International Journal of Psycho-Analysis.* 76(6): 609–618.

Stoltenberg, C.D. (1981) 'Approaching supervision from a developmental perspective', *Journal of Counselling Psychology* 28(1): 59–65.

Stoltenberg, C.D. and Delworth, U. (1987) *Supervising Counsellors and Therapists.* San Francisco and London: Jossey-Bass.

Szecsödy, I. (1990) 'Supervision: a didactic or mutative situation', Psychoanalytic Psychotherapy, 4(3): 245–261.

Yalom, I.D. (1995) *The Theory and Practice of Group Psychotherapy.* New York: Basic Books.

Chapter 7

Supervising Short-Term Psychodynamic Work

Gertrud Mander

Nothing in my dozen years of supervising long-term psychodynamic work, in groups and individually, prepared me for the task of supervising counsellors doing brief and time-limited work. This was virgin territory and I had to invent a method that allowed me to cope with the particular issues with which I found myself confronted: those of assessment, structuring, focusing, ending, loss, and, moreover, with a fast turnover of clients.

First I had to overcome a prejudice against the new fashion for short-term counselling contracts being offered to employees, in the context of Employment Assistance Programmes. Then I had to familiarise myself with a growing tendency in institutions and health authorities which aimed for modest goals and a module model for the counselling of the multitudes at the workplace, in colleges and in GP surgeries. This new development in the counselling world goes hand in hand with greater awareness of the value of therapeutic interventions and promises a much wider distribution of our wares than has been possible in the past, at the expense of orthodoxies and cherished beliefs about giving people what they need or are supposed to need. To work as a supervisor in this sector was quite a challenge for me. It promised a learning experience and a distinct possibility for helping to break down barriers of prejudice and privilege.

In the past I had received a short training in the brief focal psychotherapy model developed by Balint (1972) and Malan (1963) that had trained me to work psychodynamically with contracts of up to six months or 25 sessions, and I had become familiar with formulating a psychodynamic focus and working with the ending from the beginning. I had also looked at the time-limited model of James Mann (1973) and attended workshops given by H. Davanloo (1978) and Angela Molnos (1995), all of whom focused on concepts of time and favoured time-limited contracts. Further reading, of de Shazer (1985) and Haley (1973) proved most intriguing. So, when the invitation came to supervise a counsellor working with time-limited contracts in a GP practice and a group of counsellors for Counselling in Companies, WPF, who were working with a five-session solution-focused brief therapy model, I took my chance.

CiC is one of many employment assistance programmes (EAPs) that enable employees of large firms to receive free counselling support through their workplace. It calls on a large body of professional counsellors to whom it refers clients from the many commercial companies who use it as a service provider. The counsellors see their clients in private practice and much of supervision also happens in the private practice setting. Supervision is compulsory and free, and the supervisor is chosen for the counsellor by a clinical manager. This is a three-cornered employment relationship in which the supervisor follows the guidelines set up by the service provider who pays for the supervision work. It creates an interesting dynamic situation in which the clients can be held firmly, the counsellors feel supported and the supervisor is entrusted with the responsibility to implement the contract. However, as nobody is guaranteed ongoing work (including the supervisor) there is an uncertainty about supply and demand that may mirror the clients' employment situation while emphasising all the difficulties the self-employed counsellor in private practice experiences at a time when the profession is unable to balance supply and demand for all its members. As a CiC (EAP) supervisor I never know from one week to the next whether my services will be called for.

Five years of doing the work for CiC have made me realise that this is completely different from the analytic setting, for the supervisor and for the counsellor. Time is of the essence and the supervision space quickly fills up with people jostling each other. This kind of supervision is like watching people travel up an escalator. They are off and on in a flash and you catch no more than a glimpse of them while they are achieving the task of moving from one level to the next.

By now I have seen dozens of people do it. I briefly make their acquaintance, see them in close-up, sharply lit, then I have to let them go and turn my attention to the next person. Even the counsellors are short-term: they come when they have a case, for the space of the five sessions they have with the client, and are off again, until such time when they have been allocated another client. And, as they do with the client, we always work flexitime in supervision. Not with regard to the hour and the analytic frame, but with regard to frequency, gaps between sessions and appointment times.

There is none of the continuity and regularity of the analytic setting, where we have months or years to look at cases, and develop relationships and hypotheses with leisure. It is now or never, one week on, the next week off, fitting in with the counsellors' time as they fit in with their clients', and supporting them in the task, from the beginning to the end of their particular contracts. Scheduling, hence, becomes an art, or a headache, whichever way you look at it. As with everything to do with brief work, there is an urgency that makes one inventive: the clock is ticking, one thinks on one's toes, responds fast, finds quick solutions, does not look back and always has to hold many things in mind simultaneously, because, in the words of the poet Andrew Marvell, 'at my back I always hear, time's winged chariot hurrying near'. The end is always close in sight, awesomely pressing in on the meetings as it gets closer.

This is why some people call the brief therapy experience a near-death experience.

I have learnt that in supervising short-term work I need to carefully observe the frame. To start with I insist on hearing about all clients immediately after the first session, and carefully go over the assessment session in order to help the counsellor focus on the problem brought by the client, to understand its psychodynamic implications and to hypothesise about the goal and possible solution that can be reached in the short time allocated. We also look at first impressions and counter-transference in order to learn as much as possible about the client and to identify early on in each case what might be difficult for the counsellor.

Even more than in long-term therapy, assessment in brief work establishes quickly the future course of the treatment and of the working alliance, while its powerful impact on the clients will determine their motivation, their willingness or their defensiveness. It will open doors for them to an understanding and experience of the kind they have not known before. 'In the beginning is my end', as T.S. Eliot said. Everything will be there in a nutshell in that first session: the client's problem; the client's expectations for its solution; the client's belief and the client's disbelief in the possibility of being helped; the client's willingness to engage in the task and their anxiety about the difficulties and suffering this might entail; the client's fear about the unknown events likely to happen, and the client's uncertainty of being with a stranger whose motives and methods are unfamiliar. All this is there and needs to be harnessed, mobilised and transformed into curiosity and trust, and into a functioning working alliance that allows the work to be done and completed in a short space of time.

Assessment

Assessment is like anatomy where careful dissection of the body in the search for the probable cause of the illness leads to the making of a diagnosis on the basis of the symptoms and morbidity discovered. In scanning the client's story systematically to find the cause for the psychic turbulence and discomfort that has made them seek help, the counsellor becomes the anatomist or investigator, who tracks down a core problem, tries to read its symptoms in the light of their professional knowledge and experience of pathology, and makes a quick decision about how to contain and tackle the disturbance and how to involve the client in the task for the short period of time at their disposal. The counsellor will also test the client's suitability for counselling, their ego strength, ability to relate, to cope with strong feelings, to sustain the intense experience of exploring a dilemma that has seemed insoluble and to separate at the end of this endeavour without harm to either participant.

In supervision, after the initial assessment, the task is to deepen the findings and to examine the decisions reached, confirming or adjusting the focus envisaged and preparing carefully for the next and the following sessions. The counsellor may be uncertain about the client's suitability, ego strength and disturbance levels, overwhelmed by a wealth of material and therapeutic possibilities, longing to offer long-term work and daunted by lack of time. This requires a supervisory experience that is both challenging and supportive, firming up the knowledge that making a difference (de Shazer, 1975) is all that can be done in the short time available. The supervisor will help the counsellor set something in motion that can cause a ripple effect in the client's life, which may turn into a process of self-examination (as the psychodynamic counsellor believes) or solution behaviour (as the cognitive behaviorist calls it). A limited goal will have to be found and clear strategies discussed of how to implement it in the few sessions to come.

Sometimes the counselling may not go further than the assessment and the counsellor will have to be helped to accept this and make the session as meaningful and therapeutic as possible. At other times it may be necessary to consider a different option, a referral or a change of direction which had not occurred to the counsellor. A situation may occur when the counsellor's anxiety or defence against anxiety has produced a blind spot, as with a supervisee who ignored a client's recent traumatic bereavement and focused on her inability to enjoy life when she herself had just been diagnosed with a severe illness of her own. Another example is the frequent lament: 'this client needs long-term work'. This can be unhelpful at the beginning of a short-term contract, when the client has not yet had the chance to prove their ability for change and often demonstrates high anxiety levels which may abate as the work proceeds and may reflect the counsellor's guilt feelings about not giving them as much as they have had themselves.

At this point in the therapy anything is possible, and the participants' belief in the method can work small wonders, if the iron is struck while it is hot. The supervisor will need to defuse or take over the counsellor's anxiety by communicating their belief that something can be done that can be enough for the time being, and that on the whole a process is set in motion that will lead to change. If nothing at all happens, which in my experience is rare, then nothing will be lost – except an opportunity for the client to use an offer of help. If the work done leads to the realisation in the counsellor that the client is ready for further counselling and the client agrees to be referred on, then supervision will be used to explore the possibilities and to enable the counsellor to initiate a referral with the help of procedures developed at CiC, managing the difficult task of letting go themselves and of persuading the client that they will need to work with someone else, without feeling deprived or aggrieved.

A thorough assessment needs to be followed up by disciplined batting and fielding of the ball. The supervisor will become the guardian of the focus, once this is firmly set, and will be there to remind the counsellors when they wander off it or when their attention strays from the imperative need to keep the ending in mind. They will also monitor and contain the psychodynamics of the interaction; identifying the transference and counter-transference situation so that the therapeutic relationship can function effectively without becoming inseparable and so difficult to end that both partners wish for a continuation of the therapy.

The five-session model practised by CiC counsellors works best with one-on-one supervision, as this ensures maximum concentration and monitoring. With more experience though, the minimum requirement seems to be three supervision sessions, whether the contract is for 5, 10, 12 or 15 client sessions. James Mann (1973) divides brief therapy work into three parts and others compare it to a game of chess: beginning, middle, and end. Opening games, middle ones and end stages can be marked as in any relationship. The three stages require somewhat different supervisory input.

In the middle stage the forward and backward view allows review, prediction and limitation, an interim assessment of what has been achieved and of what still needs to be and can be done. At this point it is apparent whether the client is benefitting and the question can be legitimately asked whether they have been helped to work towards solving their problem, whether more therapy might be useful, and whether they have been initiated sufficiently into clienthood for this to be possible.

My belief in the efficacy of brief therapy modes rests on the experience that in many cases it can be an initiation into a psychological way of thinking, and hence a priming for further therapy. In my supervisory endeavour I always stress this aspect of the work, partly to lessen the counsellor's anxiety that they are not giving their clients enough, partly to remind them of the general rule that nothing is ever enough, and that all through life there are moments when even the best-analysed person might contemplate further bouts of short- or long-term work.

Ongoing supervisory tasks in brief work are:

- Concentrating on the intense counter-transference experience, the counsellor's and one's own, for diagnostic clues, ethical dangers and emotional containment.
- Modelling an active relationship. The model's active style of intervening, questioning, decision-making, an alertness, quickfootedness, preparedness, and a firm resistance to seduction, elation and dejection. Last but not least, abstinence and a stance of remaining realistic in one's goals throughout the work.
- Assisting in the necessary brief mourning, grief work and any other finishing business after the end of each contract, clearing the ground and the memory for the next beginning, attending to issues of referral, follow up and feedback.

CiC (EAP) clients come from an organisational context, where work issues and relationships can easily become a focus of psychic turbulence and hence the focus for the therapeutic work. Their particular way of object-seeking and object-relating is reflected in relationships with bosses, colleagues and employees, and their core problems can be tackled in this arena as well as in their personal situations. Helping them to withdraw projections and transferences, to see themselves as others do, to assert their rights, to plan and reduce their workload, and to manage the anxieties arising from restructuring, redundancy threat and impending retirement are tasks that can be achieved or at least started in brief work, with a view to the clients' learning new ways of looking after their own needs. In supervision these tasks can be planned, discussed and conceptualised in relation to each individual client.

In my supervisory experience of counselling at work I continually find that the client new to counselling, and perhaps rather wary of it, can best find a way into their blocked internal world by becoming aware of their unconscious contribution to blockages in the difficult work relationships they blame on others. It would be grandiose to claim that a few sessions can move them permanently from the paranoid/schizoid to the depressive position, but steps in that direction undoubtedly occur and the new experience of being able to affect and shift a seemingly hopeless work situation can be one of those momentous steps. In other words, they may be helped to start on their journey of individuation, which involves being more self-aware and less in need of projecting their own unwanted bits onto others.

Reinforcing such experiences of potency both for the counsellor and client can be done in supervision, but the opportunity for a repeated working through of a stuck position is, of course, what the model lacks and the advocates of brief work may have underestimated its importance. It may be too early to expect conclusive research and outcome studies concerning relapse or referral-on rates, and in my opinion not enough work is done on providing follow-ups or repeated contracts. However, the success of the Malan model, which includes follow-ups over extended periods of time, and of the CAT model which allows repeats, may be a pointer to the future, when short-term work may become a form of successive contracting.

In supervising counsellors in GP practices and student counsellors, I experience some interesting differences from the CiC/EAP supervision due to client populations and organisational contexts, which demand a different supervisory style. Both contexts offer the clients an environment in which they are held and they develop transferences to a number of people, in particular doctors and tutors. The counsellor receives self-referrals or referrals from colleagues and sees the clients on the premises, while CiC/EAP counsellors operate from home. This means both more or less containment, depending on whether it is a GP practice or an educational setting and on organisational size, atmosphere and trust, and on the split or shared transferences which can support or undermine the counselling work. Also, clients tend to be more transitory and often attend no more than one session, disappearing after an assessment that established crisis and pathology levels beyond the powers of the counsellor to contain. Or they come and go, as they please, as long as they are attached to the setting. If they are practice patients this may be over many years, if they are students, over the duration of their course, yet mostly not in the holidays, which rules out long-term work.

Supervising this kind of short-term work is different and difficult, because most of it consists of one-off consulting, focusing on assessment, diagnosis, suitability or frame issues. GP clients tend to be somatisers, the worried well, or patients with various chronic diseases. Student clients suffer from specific stresses like leaving home, exam or social phobias, crises and breakdowns triggered off by isolation and separation issues characteristic of prolonged adolescence. They seem to be the most difficult clients to engage and induct into the regular, once weekly rhythm and hence provoke particular anxieties in their counsellors to do with uncertainty, feeling let down or rejected, disappointed or frustrated. Often the counsellor's supervisory needs are not met because of lack of funding and generally they feel undervalued and marginalised by their employers which becomes a regular subject for complaint in supervision where organisational issues can take over and swamp the session, to the detriment of the clinical work. The supervisor needs to resist the pull of getting sidetracked and drawn into the counsellor's personal authority issues, to watch out for and monitor the extent to which the organisation dwarfs everything else, as this can reflect imbalances and resistances in client, counsellor and supervisor, and be counterproductive to any creative work. It can also be helpful to analyse the organisational dynamics which get taken on by the counsellor.

An area that requires special attention in these two contexts is the multicultural dimension which is more often encountered in these settings as clients from different ethnic groups are less likely to find the private practice way into counselling, and are more likely to avail themselves of the free counselling service offered by both settings. Also they are likely to be referred by authority figures like doctors and college staff, and hence present the 'sent' syndrome, a combination of compliance and reluctance with which it is difficult to work, particularly for inexperienced counsellors of whom there are quite a few, as these settings are used for placements required by many counselling courses.

What concerns the supervisor in relation to the multi-ethnicity of these client populations is their sensitivity to issues of prejudice and discrimination, and the counsellors' denial or apprehensiveness of these. I maintain that these issues are still rarely tackled firmly enough and that they need to be put into words as soon as possible, as they belong to the first impression each participant has of the other, and will always influence the client's decision whether or not to enter into the counselling relationship, and colour their resistance and the counsellor's counter-resistance. These issues can also become the main creative focus of the work, but generally require the sensitive handling that any problem of difference demands.

There is a decisive difference between the short-term work of the counsellor whose inexperience considers the work finished at the first indication of a client's feeling better or expressing a desire to stop, and the short-term counsellor who uses the honeymoon period at the beginning of therapy to maximum effect, structuring the contract around this and defining the therapeutic space in advance. Beginners invariably mistake flight into health for change and mishandle the onset of ambivalence. Everybody is aware that doing short-term work requires skill and experience of assessment, a well-developed technique and knowledge of the potential of what can be done (and not done). The supervisor has to supply this experience when it is lacking in the counsellor and teach the rudiments of technique by constantly reiterating the basics and rigorously holding the counsellor to the task. There is a constant need to assess the counsellor, too, and if necessary counsellors have to be told in supervision that they haven't got it in them to do short-term work. This can be due to an inability to let go, to contain the transference, to curb the client's desire to become dependent, or simply to make quick decisions, to think on their feet and to work fast which is necessary for this sort of work. This is not surprising. Not every client benefits from brief therapy, and, equally, not every counsellor wants to or is able to work in this mode. It may follow that not every supervisor can or wants to supervise it. There are pack horses and race horses ...

Whether it is done in a group or individually, this kind of supervision demands that often more than one client is discussed in a session, and this means a supervisory style that is flexible and focused. To call it 'bite-sized' might be accurate, but this does not mean hurried or superficial, rather more active and concentrated than supervision of long-term casework or of training cases. I guess the secret is to focus on the counsellor and on the counter-transference, and to trust that the unconscious process of reflections and par-allels will guide and activate one's intuition and thinking. Of course, much is left out and once chosen one has to follow an avenue of thought to wherever it leads. The maxim in short-term work is that there is only one chance.

As a clinical example I have chosen a fairly typical session with a student counsellor who comes fortnightly to supervision, which may illustrate the work.

The student counsellor comes first thing in the morning before going to work and we both have to make an effort to get up early. She starts out with her own rather difficult domestic situation in order to clear her mind for the task. It is a marital problem and may require her to set a condition. Having established that, we move on to a past case from her small private practice where there is an issue of unset-tled fees, which requires her to write a firm letter. Then she talks briefly about a colleague at work who has 'absolutely no boundaries' and has asked her for an appointment to discuss some work and personal problems. After talking about this for a while the counsellor understands that this is inappropriate and itself a boundary problem and that the colleague needs to be helped to find a counsellor external to the college.

Next, she says she has many clients at the moment. Who to start with? There is the man who came to talk about his relationship problems and whom she finds sexually exciting. He missed the last session and she feels that he wants her to ask him to come back. What does this tell her about his problems and his seductive ploys? Pondering this, she says, 'Now I know what to do', and moves on to another student who is German, but has excellent English and talks so fast that she says she has to 'get on her bicycle' to follow her. The client is an ex-drug addict and is doing a course in nursery nursing. She talks in a mechanical sort of way like a textbook, like vomiting over the counsellor. All she can do is keep up with the flow of words, trying to follow a complex and chaotic story, but she cannot think nor focus on anything. It reminds me of how she feels about her domestic situation, and I realise that this is a reflection process. I try to help her identify a problem in the client's material that could be solved and hence could become the focus of the work. When I mention solution talk she brightens up and can now attend to the material in a creative way focusing on the client's entanglement with her mother and with the parents of her boyfriend who was killed in a fatal accident She realises that the client's problem is that she needs to disentangle herself and suddenly understands that she herself needs to do the same thing. 'I have to set a condition', she says hopefully as she gathers up her things. It feels as if she has understood one of the fundamentals of brief work which applies to all the different situations she has brought to this session.

Note

This chapter was first published in *Counselling*, 9(4): 301–305.

References

Balint, M. (1972) *Focal Psychotherapy, An Example of Applied Psychoanalysis*. London: Tavistock Publications.

Davanloo, H. (ed.) (1978) *Basic Principles and Techniques in Short-Term Dynamic Therapy*. New York: Spectrum.

de Shazer, S. (1975) *Keys to Solution in Brief Therapy*. New York: Norton.

Haley, J. (1973) *Uncommon Therapy: The Psychiatric Techniques of Milton H. Erickson*. New York: Norton.

Malan D.H. (1963) *A Study of Brief Psychotherapy*. London: Tavistock Publications.

Mann, J. (1973) *Time-Limited Psychotherapy*. Cambridge, MA and London: Harvard University Press.

Molnos, A. (1995) *A Question of Time*. London: Karnac Books.

Chapter 8

The Container and the Contained: Supervision and its Organisational Context

John Stewart

Human beings need to establish organisational structures to achieve social cohesion and promote a sense of psychological and economic well being. Individuals have been part of a family group, have been subjected to the pressures of educational institutions, they have been employed in organisations, affiliated to a variety of social groupings such as clubs or religious bodies and subjected to the organisational infrastructure of politics and government. The provision of psychotherapy will often be dependent on political and statutory organisations for funding and therefore be subject to political policy and public audit for the way it carries out its practice.

The practitioners of psychodynamic psychotherapy and counselling ignore the organisational dimension at their peril, as it is always present in their work. All three participants (supervisor, supervisee and patient) in the supervisory triangle bring their own organisational history to the supervisory situation and each has to exist within the institutional structure that underpins their work.

Supervisors relate to organisations in differing ways according to the setting of the work. Supervisors may be employed within the same organisation as their supervisees, they may be hired as an outside consultant by an institution, they may be employed as a training supervisor in a training body, or may work on a private basis. Both supervisor and supervisee will probably belong to professional organisations under whose codes of ethics they will practice. The balance as to which organisation the supervisee and supervisor are accountable and to whom a supervisee or patient may have recourse to complain, will vary from situation to situation.

These issues are highlighted in the following scenario, used as a whole group exercise, in training for psychodynamic supervisors.

The scenario is that a relatively large organisation offering counselling services is faced with a financial crisis. Income is generated through fees negotiated on the basis of the client's ability to pay. As a training organisation it is in receipt of trainee fees and the work of counsellors and psychotherapists in training who are unpaid. On balance the organisation has to service a planned deficit through fund raising and grant applications, as many clients are unwaged and therefore pay low fees.

The Director and the Financial Manager have made a decision to streamline the services offered by closing a department and making redundancies. It has also decided that an approach will be made to all clients asking them to consider increasing the fee they pay, in negotiation with their therapist. The Director has written to each client personally in a standardised letter to explain the situation. The situation was discussed with groups of supervisors, the managers of whom indicated that following discussion in supervision, the letter is to be handed to the client by the counsellor within a three-week period. Counsellors and supervisors were notified that the decision had been made and would have to be implemented.

The group exercise was set up in the following way with several successive cohorts of trainee supervisors. Members were assigned the roles of director, clinical manager, supervisor (in a group of three), supervisee/therapist and patient and placed in different rooms. A receptionist was put in place. Group members were detailed to 'shadow' each role to observe what occurs and to monitor the feelings evoked through their own identification with that role. One person was instructed to follow the process as a silent observer. The communication was set in motion to 'travel,' from the director, to the supervisors group (via the clinical manager), into the supervision session, and onto the patient and to subsequently to 'return', via the reverse process, as feedback to the director. Five minutes is allocated to each encounter and 45 minutes for the ensuing whole group discussion.

In the discussion that follows, I describe participants as being in a specific role in a group exercise or place their title in inverted commas to indicate that they are playing out that role. The plural is used because reference is being made to several people who have played the same role.

The organisation as a functioning system

The operational complexities of organisations and the way in which they impact on supervision are difficult to unravel. Some useful models on which to base our thinking about organisational functioning are based on the use of analogy. The first explores an organisation's interaction with the environment through the biological analogy with an organism, while the second uses the psychological analogy with the structure of the human psyche. The basis for this discussion is drawn from the collection of papers edited by deBoard (1978).

Organisation as an organism

Put simply, an organism has to interact with its environment in order to maintain its existence. An efficient energy flow needs to be maintained so that resources are drawn from the environment, made usable through internal processes, and output to the environment is generated. Such output makes an impact on the environment. One aspect of such impact is to ensure survival by promoting the ongoing supply of resources. This is defined as an open system of functioning.

Changing environmental conditions require an organism to adapt its structure to survive. Failure to respond to change will result, as in the case of the dinosaurs, in cataclysmic extinction. When the capacity of an organism to interact with the environment becomes moribund it degenerates into what is defined as a closed system of functioning.

Even without the threat of sudden extinction organisms have a finite existence – they grow old and die, although the survival of the species, given favourable environmental conditions, is ensured by reproduction.

Organisations too, are required to interact with their environment as open systems. Failure to maintain an adequate system of input, process and output will lead to the formation of a closed system and eventual termination of functioning. History provides many examples such as the Industrial Revolution or the recent development of Information Technology, which led to the decline of established organisations and vocational groupings.

Organisations progress through what could be called 'life stages' or developmental stages. The structural shape will evolve from the need for innovation and improvisation, through a need to consolidate and on to a need to terminate or evolve a new structure. The leadership attributes required of key personnel will also evolve. The charismatic innovator will not easily co-exist with the ongoing need to consolidate and be a safe pair of hands. Neither style will feel comfortable with a leadership style that is required to make radical decisions about restructuring the organisation or even to close it down.

A supervisor in a new organisation may be required to work flexibly and to develop procedures as the organisation evolves. Initially a supervisor may have to work concurrently with a variety of roles such as supervisor, tutor and even therapist, but as an organisation matures and develops the role of the supervisor will become more defined.

The supervisor has to ensure that what they do in supervision functions as an open system which has a discrete process of input, process and output. Supervision engages two interfacing encounters between supervisor and supervisee and between therapist and patient, each of which maintains a cycle of input, process and output. The task of the supervisor is to monitor the process of the therapeutic interaction between therapist and patient to ensure that the needs of the patient are being appropriately met. At the same time the supervisor must be alive to the dynamics of the supervisory relationship – what does the supervisee bring to the session, how is this processed in supervision and how is this used in the ongoing work with the patient?

The supervisor also has a responsibility to monitor the extent to which the supervisee works in a way which is consistent with the aims and needs of the organisation. If, for example, a supervisee is engaged in long term work in a organisation which is needing to conduct time limited work as part of its overall strategy, then clearly something is happening which is against the best interests of the organisation. It may help the particular patient but work against the organisation's best interests.

Clinical discussion

In the example under discussion the 'supervisors' were faced with input additional to the task of supervising ongoing work with the patient. The input had an effect on the 'supervisior' in that the initial sense of shock was followed by an expression of anger and, usually, a recovery of thought as to what needed to be done. 'Supervisees' reported a similar reaction when the news was broken to them. Some 'patients' drew attention to their own financial crises such as redundancy. 'Supervisors' all spoke of their anxiety about having to balance conflicting demands. Some were able to discuss with the supervisee the possibility of a temporary deferal of the increase in fee until the patient was in a better financial position, or to think about taking the difficulty back to management for further discussion.

The analogy with the human psyche

This analogy shifts the point of attention to the internal process of organisations. According to this model a well-functioning individual has a reasonable sense of their own identity and sufficient ego strength to manage transactions both with their environment and their own internal process. The ego of the individual will therefore maintain a measure of control over their own boundary functions, with the result that they react appropriately to the impact of outside stimuli on their bodily and mental functioning and respond in a way which furthers their own survival. In other words they can act and think appropriately.

The internal mental processes of the individual will include the capacities to attend to several tasks at once, to prioritise the necessity to act and to adapt their personal functioning in order to meet changing conditions in the external world. A well-functioning individual demonstrates an ability to cope with more primitive instinctual need so that, if action is prioritised, gratification can be postponed and frustration tolerated. A capacity to be aware of the unconscious dimension of many of their actions and to monitor the effect of their personal defences against anxiety and stress, considerably augment their survival skills.

If we allow for the fact that no analogy is exact, we can use the example of personal functioning as an analogy for the ways in which organisations work. An effective management structure will, ego like, perform several important organisational tasks. It will maintain organisational boundaries with the external world in terms of input and output. Management will define the overall objectives of the organisation and reach decisions as to how this is to be implemented. Effective management is thus 'task centred'. Part of the task performance is to establish an effective internal structure so that the roles of individuals and sub-systems will be defined in a way which minimises conflict and boundary skirmishing and facilitates the management of the component parts of the organisation. Objectives will be defined and priorities established in the service of the overall task.

Individuals within the organisation have a need to know what is expected of them, to feel some affirmation for task performance from their superiors, to know they are properly remunerated and to believe their input into the shape of the organisation is at least given some credence.

On a personal level the individual is required to be able to interact with others, to hold focus on a task and prioritise actions taken to achieve their designated tasks. In other words to contribute to the overall task performance of the organisation.

Supervisors have to be mindful that they do not operate in isolation and are required to hold an awareness of many other roles and functions held and performed within an organisation. Finance, training, intake, publicity, personnel management and so on, all contribute to the whole body and service the operation of more specialised functions such as supervision.

It is also crucial that the space for supervising is not imperiled by the over-intrusion of organisational pressure. This dilemma requires the supervisor to exercise good judgement in relation to the balance of need between the integrity of the therapeutic process and the input of 'external' information. Thought has to be given as to what information is appropriate to introduce into the supervision session and also to the timing of when this should be done. At times supervisor and supervisee may be required to think about similar issues in relation to the supervisee's work with the patient.

Clinical discussion

In the example under discussion, the 'supervisors' had to bear in mind the overall needs of the organisation. They had to accept that the instruction of the 'director' and figures provided by the 'financial manager' were in the best interests of the organisation and within the remit of its defined task. They usually expressed shock and initial anger about the manner in which they were told. They did have an opportunity to discuss the matter and express their feelings in the 'supervisors' group. Such a grouping was always reported to be supportive. Discussing the matter with the 'supervisee' often produced a feeling of panic about their capacity to contain the anxiety of the 'supervisee' about the state of the organisation and help them to think about how they would handle the situation with the patient. The supervisor also had to be mindful of the impact on the patient. Some 'supervisors' felt enraged and over-identified with the client. Others expressed feelings about colleagues being made redundant, which they were tempted to disclose to the 'supervisee'.

It is interesting that the 'director' and the 'finance manager' often felt increasingly anxious as time went on. The reaction which was taken back to them was usually a strong one which focused on the way the issue had been handled, rather than the overall situation in which the organisation found itself.

The clinical rhombus

The concept of the clinical rhombus (Ekstein and Wallerstein, 1958), with its four points of supervisor (S) therapist supervisee (T), patient (P) and administrator (A), brings the specific interface between supervision and the organisation into consideration (see Figures 8.1 and 8.2). All interface potentially with each other except for the supervisor and patient. 'Administrator' may indicate a specific management role or it may represent a part of the administrative function, for instance, a financial officer or the receptionist.

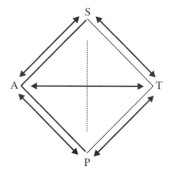

FIGURE 8.1   *Interactions in the clinical rhombus*

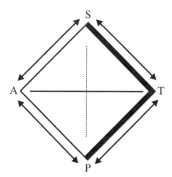

FIGURE 8.2   *Intensity of interactions in the clinical rhombus*

If one could imagine the lines thickening according to the intensity of connection, the thickest lines would between therapist and patient and (T–P) and the supervisor and therapist (S–T). The administrator will have connections with the supervisor (A–S) as they are paid a fee, they will have some contact with the therapist (A–T) as they will have to negotiate over the availability of consulting rooms, take in the fee paid by the patient, and they may have some dealings with the patient (A–P) regarding assessment interviews, although contact is minimal once therapy has commenced. There is no overt connection between the supervisor and the patient (S–P).

Clinical discussion

In the situation outlined in the letter from the 'director' the intensity of communication of Administration was increased with all other points of the rhombus. Organisational issues were writ large as 'managers' and 'finance officers' exercised their authority but trainees in this role expressed anxiety and paranoid feelings about what was happening in the rest of organisation. In the A–P axis there was an increased potential anxiety in the 'patient'. Some trainees in the role of 'patients' responded in an anxious way fearful of the organisation's future, others agreed to a rise in the level of fee with apparent concern. The impact on the A–S axis had the effect of increasing the level of concern in the supervisors' mind, but they had to form a judgement as to what material would be appropriate to pass on to the supervisee in the S–T link. The 'receptionist' as the visible but powerless face of the administration picked up the discontent of the 'patient' and the 'therapist' and was, in some instances, surprised by the increased level of anxiety the 'supervisor' revealed.

The extended clinical rhombus

The clinical rhombus still remains a durable and useful device for thinking about the supervisory setting. Its limitation, in my view, lies in the static nature of the construction. It draws attention to the conscious functioning of the four points of the rhombus, but it is less able to represent the constantly shifting complexities of the supervisory setting. I wish to attempt to illustrate this complexity by extending the clinical rhombus into an elongated cube with an articulated joint in the middle which allows it to rotate like a Rubik's cube on one of its axes (see Figure 8.3). One half of the cube remains static while the other can rotate. The static end of the cube represents the interaction of the defined roles at a conscious level of thinking. The rotating end of the cube represents the fluctuating and oscillating potential for identification, which any of the parties may have with the other three points of the rhombus. Such identifications may be based on past or present experience in other organisations which may or may not have been therapeutic in nature.

The supervisor will identify with the supervisory role (S–S). The supervisor will have been supervised and will therefore identify with the supervisee (S–T). The supervisor will have been a patient and will identify with the patient (P–T). The supervisor may also have administrative skills and hold views on the efficacy of management (S–A). The supervisee or therapist may have a similar range of identifications. The patient will have, at the very least, views about organisational efficiency. A multiplicity of role is most pronounced in an organisaton offering training.

Triangle of involvement

It would be helpful to extend the discussion beyond the dynamics represented by the rhombus. The scope is widened so that attention moves backwards to

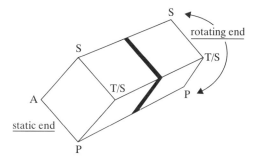

FIGURE 8.3 *The extended clinical rhombus*

participants' 'organisational history' and outwards to current organisational involvement beyond the supervisory setting. In order to provide a frame of reference in which to examine the wider perspective, I advance the notion of the triangle of involvement. This is an adaptation of Malan's triangle of person (Malan, 1997) that is a useful model through which the operation of the transference in therapy sessions is represented (see Figure 8.4). In the triangle of person, T represents work in the transference in the here and now of the therapy session. O represents other relationships usually current or in the recent past. P represents relationships with the parents or sibling usually in the distant past.

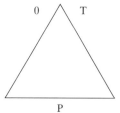

FIGURE 8.4 *Triangle of person*

All the participants in the supervisory endeavour have a personal history of involvement with organisations and all have a complex network of organisational influences in the current therapeutic context. In adapting the triangle of person to the triangle of involvement (see Figure 8.5) I endeavour to provide a framework in which to think about this complexity.

The S represents the ongoing interactions of supervision as represented by the clinical rhombus. The O point represents involvement in organisational activity which is either current or in the recent past and would include such things as a personal relationship or present family unit, social and religious groupings, and the wider social and political spheres in which all participants live. The participants will carry all manner of hopes, expectations and fears relating to other organisational experience into the present situation. Expectations regarding the outcome of therapy from the patient's family, or relating

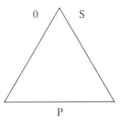

FIGURE 8.5   *Triangle of involvement*

to the perceived performance of the organisation by bodies making referrals, providing funding or making social policy, bring outside pressure to bear on therapeutic endeavour.

P represents the organisational experience which the participants bring from their distant past in their family of origin or early educational and social groupings. Feelings relating to dependency and autonomy, inclusion and exclusion, envy and jealousy will be carried from past relationships and formative stages of development into their modes of relating in the current organisational setting.

Unconscious processes in organisations

Supervision provides a forum in which supervisee and supervisor can pay careful attention to the material the patient brings to the therapy session. The supervisor may also note ways in which the patient's material is unconsciously reflected in the supervisee's presentation. The supervisor however is not working as a therapist and it is unhelpful to draw direct attention to or foster the transference evoked between supervisor and supervisee. Such transference always exists, organisational issues constantly influence it, and, while it may have to be acknowledged, it is detrimental to the task of supervision to indulge in interpretation.

Supervisors need to be aware of the personal transference's evoked in organisational dynamics and to find appropriate avenues in which to resolve their own issues. They may communicate their concerns about organisational issues to an appropriate person in a management position but, unless they have a management role, they may have to deal with organisational anxiety as best they can at a supervisory level in order to preserve the effectiveness of the supervisee's work with the patient.

Earlier in the paper an analogy was made between the psychodynamic model of the human psyche and the management function in an organisation, but the analogy was incomplete in so far as it did not address the impact of unconscious dynamics on organisational processes. Organisations are suffused with unconscious feelings.

A significant element in feelings and thoughts about an organisation is the perception as to the extent to which it can act as a container for the anxiety, which besets those who work within it. The more intense the level of anxiety the more people are prone to revert to primitive levels of functioning in an attempt to defend themselves against feelings of inadequacy or personal disintegration. Defences against anxiety are manifested in a variety of forms which range from neurotic thinking about guilt or blame to early and more primitive modes of functioning. Anna Freud (1986) conceptualises a range of such defenses as psychological mechanisms but the framework developed by Melanie Klein shifts the focus to a 'position' of defence first employed in early infancy. Adults under duress retreat to very early methods of defending themselves against anxiety and, in the context of this discussion, this would include stress induced by organisational pressures.

Klein (1975) defined these early defences as the paranoid–schizoid position. This is paranoid in the sense that the self, when subject to excessively impinging or persecuting forces which threaten the sense of internal cohesion, reacts in a schizoid manner leading to a split perception of reality. Individuals cope with excessive anxiety by projecting unwanted feelings into another person. The most extreme form of projection is projective identification through which the recipient of the projection becomes identified as being more or less identical to the sum of the projections. In a state of extreme anxiety feelings projected into figures in the external world lead to the perception of the other as either a good or bad object. Internal objects are therefore based on the external world but because of the distorting effect of unconscious phantasy, they may be caricatures of reality.

Klein describes the achievement of the depressive position as the goal of personal integration and the basis of a healthy mental state. The dawning of the realisation that the other is both the good and bad object and therefore the recipient of feelings of love and hate leads to the depressing realisation that one can damage that which one loves. The ability to make reparation, to care for others and be cared for by them is built on this foundation. The capacity to hold ambivalent feelings about others and to tolerate mixed feelings about oneself are a feature of the depressive position. Klein uses the term 'position' to indicate that the depressive position is not a once and for all developmental milestone but a state of mind towards which we work and from which we 'backslide' into more primitive ways of functioning. States of high anxiety push individuals towards the paranoid–schizoid position but it is the rate at which 'recovery' to the depressive position is achieved which indicates the achievement of adequate emotional maturity.

The identity of an organisation is defined by its title and is linked to the external reality of bricks and mortar, but it exists fundamentally in the mind of the individual members as a good or bad internal object or one about which there are mixed feelings. A well-functioning organisation is one in which there is a sufficient commonality of ideals between individual members and that this is shaped by maintaining clear and updated organisational aims. It is also the case that the forces of organisational interaction produce a prevailing culture, which is somewhat analogous to the personality of the individual, in that the sum often does seem to be greater than its parts.

Organisations providing counselling and psychotherapy, by the very nature of their task, contain a great amount of anxiety. They are subject to external pressures to do with referrals and funding, they have to manage internal organisational pressures through maintaining effective structures, and they are subject to the unremitting demand to meet the needs of the patients. In organisations offering training the anxiety of those seeking qualification will add to the intensity of the projection to which the organisation is subjected.

The tendency to revert to primitive levels of functioning is constant. A culture of blame can develop so that perceived ills can be projected onto external bodies, other departments within the organisation, or fellow workers. Individuals become preoccupied with their own survival and can either lose sight of the task of the organisation or become actively anti-task in the way in which they behave. Menzies-Lyth (1988) describes the patterns of behaviour through which members of a school of nursing defended themselves against anxiety by devices such as blaming superiors, denigrating subordinates, and engaging in ritualistic behaviour. Her findings can be usefully adapted to organisations in which therapists are supervised.

For the purposes of this discussion it is enough to say that individuals have the potential to behave both regressively and progressively in organisations. Del Pozo (1997) adapts the concept of the depressive position to postulate a learning position. She argues that the increased levels of anxiety evoked by learning new skills or ideas cause a reversion to paranoid–schizoid defence mechanisms. It may be helpful to argue for a 'functioning position' in the attempt to understand organisational behaviour. Such a position would demand a level of ego functioning that keeps the task of the organisation in mind, shows an awareness of role function, an ability to hold boundaries, to negotiate with others and to prioritise action. It would also demand a capacity to monitor behaviour of self and others when a tendency to revert to the paranoid–schizoid position becomes manifest.

Clinical discussion

Participants in the group exercise consistently report an emotional surge towards paranoid–schizoid mental functioning. They felt isolated and blamed and experienced the organisation as uncaring and 'bad'. They were put in a position of having to pass on information that will inflict emotional discomfort on others and their anxiety increased as they expected to become the recipient of blame and attack.

'Director', 'clinical manager', 'supervisor, 'supervisee' and 'patient' all reported variations on this theme. The receptionist felt the most acute anxiety as they were subject to a variety of comments without adequate input as to what was occurring. It was a real struggle to move from a position of having 'power' inflicted upon them to a position of finding a sense of personal authority which included taking responsibility for thinking about the needs of the organisation as a whole. Some reported a temptation to stay in a position of recrimination and blame.

Another feature was a deep-seated anxiety about the survival of the organisation. Negotiations around the increase in fee often seemed to relate to primitive fears about the survival of the object although there was some indication of more reparative 'depressive position' levels of thinking.

Basic assumption groups

Bion's (1961/1968) formulations about group behaviour provide another model with which to view organisational behaviour. He postulated a dichotomy between the collaborative function of what he called a work group and the regressive tendency to form what he called basic assumption groups. There are three such basic assumption groups. A *dependency group* focuses on the needs of its members and is dominated by a leader whose designated task is to ensure those needs are met at all costs even if this threatens the purpose for which the group was formed. If a new leader fails to meet expectations they may lose their authority. A fight or flight group mobilises defences to ward off the threat of or to flee from a perceived enemy. The group may cohere around the activity of the fight or flight while avoiding any purposeful pursuit of work group behaviour. The fight/flight mechanism can operate in a group and a member may be expelled as the 'enemy within'. The *pairing group* acts on the assumption that the leader will pair with an outsider or a member of the group to provide a solution to difficulties.

The implicit hierachy of the supervisory setting is open to the enacting of basic assumption behaviour. Patterns of dependency can emerge. Supervisees may have powerful wishes to be looked after by a figure who will sort everything out for them. Supervisors can fall prey to their own omnipotence as a defence against their own uncertainty and anxiety.

Supervisor and supervisee can fall into a fight/flight pattern of behaviour in which underlying anxiety is projected onto another figure within the organisation or onto an external organisation. In group supervision a group member may be victimised as a threat to the functioning of the group.

The propensity to pair could lead a supervisor and supervisee into a collusive twosome. Subtle and unconscious group pressure to conceive a solution may thus be acted out. This is more obvious in the dynamics of a group supervision in which the supervisor and a supervisee or two supervisees form a pairing. Such a twosome may well begin to break the boundaries of the work by discussing patient material outside supervision sessions. They may develop a special relationship of mentor and protégé which contributes to a sense of jealousy and competitiveness among their peers. In some cases a personal relationship may evolve resulting in the blurring of personal and professional boundaries. This has inevitable ramifications on the process of supervision and on the functioning of the organisation.

Clinical discussion

An examination of the vignette quoted on p. 106 reveals the possibility of basic assumption activity. Some participants in the training exercise in the role of supervisor reported a sense of over identification with the supervisee and an impulse to become protective to the point of issuing instructions as to how the patient will be handled. Some supervisees reported a powerful pull towards a compliant and helpless stance. The group exercise often produced a fight/flight reaction. The supervisee and supervisor adopted a policy of non-compliance and resistance to the directive. Such a stance often assumed the patient was not in a position to express their own view and that there was no possibility of not increasing the fee in individual cases. Thoughts of leaving the organisation crossed some participants' minds. A fear that the patient may leave was also expressed.

The impact of projective identification on organisational functioning

Moylan sets out the manner in which the impact of projective identification can affect institutions and organisations: 'by knowing about the ways in which the institution can become "infected" by the difficulties and defences of their particular client group, staff are more likely to be aware when this is happening and to use their feelings to tackle their problems in a direct and appropriate way, rather than resorting to violence and despair' (1994/1998: 59). Particular patient groups can unconsciously project their dysfunctionality into staff groups who work with them. For example those working with adults with learning difficulties have to take account of an organisational tendency to become disabled in their team work. Obholzer and Roberts (1994/1998) deal with examples of the dangers of contagion in a number of specialist professional settings.

Supervision provides the thinking space and necessary containment for supervisees and as such it is the bulwark for functional sanity of the organisation. An aspect of the supervisory setting that is often neglected is the provision of an opportunity for regular and planned supervision of supervision or at least for collaborative discussion between supervisors.

Clinical discussion

It would be all too easy for the therapist to feel they have to be the great provider under the pressure of the deluge of unrequited need that exists in the client group as represented. This is particularly so in organisations with histories that derive from the pastoral or medical worlds. In the example given the patient may have formed a strong attachment not only to the therapist but also to the room, the setting and possibly support staff such as receptionists. The organisation and its visible setting becomes a significant internal object for patients. The organisation as well as the therpaist become the recipient of the hopes and disappointments the patient experiences in the therapeutic process. Boundaries have to be set, breaks in the work endured, and frustrations around arrangements survived. In the various group exercises that have been conducted on the supervision training, trainee supervisors have struggled to talk about the 'double whammy' impact of expectation that the patient projects into the therapist and, through the supervisee to the supervisor.

The supervisee and supervisor may have been drawn to a particular organisation through their own needs which may be projected onto the organisation. In the example given the supervisor had to manage and contain their own anxiety about the future of the organisation as well as dealing with the supervisee who is prone to their own organisational projections.

Conclusion

In this chapter I have set out to look at some of the issues which arise in the interface between an organisation and those who supervise therein. I began with a more functional analysis of organisational behaviour and moved on to look at unconscious manifestations of organisational dynamics to which the process of supervision is subjected. Organisations that provide psychotherapy and counselling, by their very nature, contain a great deal of mental pain and personal anxiety. The process of supervision provides a space for thinking about work with patients in which feelings can be processed and understood more fully. It is also a place in which supervisees can recover their perspective. As such it provides an important function in protecting the organisation from becoming too heavily infected by the projections to which it is subjected. Supervision needs the support of the organisation in order to function but competent supervision is a vital component of an effective organisation.

References

Bion, W. (1961/1968) *Experiences in Groups*. London: Tavistock.
deBoard, R. (1978) *The Psychoanalysis of Organisations* London and New York: Tavistock/Routledge.
dcl Pozo, M. (1997) '*On the process of supervison in psychoanalytical psychotherapy*', in B. Matindale (ed.), *Supervision and its Vicissitudes*. London: Karnac Books. pp. 39–60.
Ekstein, R. and Wallerstein, R. (1958) *The Learning and Teaching of Psychotherapy*. London: Imago.
Freud, A. (1986) *The Ego and Mechanisms of Defence*. London: Hogarth Press.
Klein, M. (1975) '*Notes on some schizoid mechanisms*', in M. Klein (ed.), *Envy and Gratitude and Other Works*. London: Hogarth Press. pp. 1–24.
Malan, D. (1997) *Individual Psychotherapy and the Science of Psychodynamics* Oxford: Butterworth Heinemann.
Menzies-Lyth, I. (1988) The functiong of social systems as a defence against anxiety, in I. Menzies-Lyth (ed.), *Containing Anxiety in Institutions. Selected Essays*. London: Free Association Books. pp. 43–98.

Moylan, D. (1994/1998) 'The dangers of contagion: projective identification processes in institutions', in A. Obholzer and V. Roberts (eds.), *The Unconscious at Work*. London and New York: Routledge. pp. 51–59.

Obholzer, A. and Roberts, V. (eds) (1994/1998) *The Unconscious at Work*. London and New York: Routledge.

PART IV

GENERIC ISSUES IN SUPERVISION

Chapter 9

Giving, Taking, Stealing: the Ethics of Supervision

Edward Martin

To commit an offence against a code of ethics is to commit an act of theft. Theft, 'the unlawful taking away of another's personal goods with the intention of converting them for one's own use' (Cassell: 1979) implies the abuse of power.

Therapeutic theft comes in many shapes and sizes. Occasionally grand theft is reported and makes waves within particular professional communities. There will be many reasons why some such thefts are not reported, the most frequent being that patients feel, as is often the case with abuse, that they were somehow at fault. Certain thefts will never be reported because simply the patient does not recognise that anything has been stolen. Other examples of theft are known because the incident is reported anecdotally usually after the patient has left the therapist and taken its place among unofficially reported incidents that tend to discredit the profession. The rationalisation that 'it might be to do with the transference' disguises the seriousness of some of these misdeeds.

Examples of therapeutic theft are:

- The 'theft of a safe container': interruptions, changes of time or place, working beyond the therapist's training and experience.
- The 'theft of fantasy' or the 'theft of inner world drama': concretising or sexualising the therapeutic relationship; the imposition of the therapist's concerns by offering opinions or issuing didactic instructions.

The British Association for Psychoanalytic and Psychodynamic Supervision and the British Association for Counselling and Psychotherapy are, to the writer's knowledge, the only two organisations in the UK that publish a Code of Ethics for Supervisors. While other organisations may make reference to 'trainees' in their codes of ethics, BAPPS's and BACP's codes of ethics address issues relating to the supervision of both trained and trainee therapists.

Codes of Ethics are designed to protect the vulnerable. One reason why patients become vulnerable in therapy is because they regress. In Chapter 1 reference is made to regression in supervision because supervision as well as therapy affects the inner world and changes the inner objects of the supervisee. While regression in supervision should be less marked than in therapy, it still remains an important aspect of psychodynamic supervision. Reliance (and therefore possibly regression) may be more pronounced in the transference between supervisees and supervisors when supervisees have completed their therapy and are relying on supervision to keep them in touch with their patient's and their own inner worlds. Thus, the BAPPS's Code of Ethics for Supervisors includes clauses that cover the supervisor/supervisee dyad and the supervisor/supervisee/patient triad.

Theft in supervision shares close similarities to theft in therapy and as most of the examples of therapeutic theft mentioned above relate to supervision as well they will now be considered in more detail from the supervisory perspective.

Possibly the most insidious form of supervisory theft is the theft of the safe container. It often occurs when supervision is taken less seriously than therapy. Reported examples of this type of theft are when supervisors eat their breakfast or lunch during the supervision session, take telephone calls, drink coffee or allow estate agents to look around the property, appearing to generally care less about boundaries than (hopefully) they would as therapists. One trainee experienced a range of conflicts when his training supervisor consistently kept him waiting past his appointment time; sitting in the waiting room the trainee could hear telephone calls being made during what was meant to be his supervision time. He felt anger and relief; anger that he was not being given the time he paid for, relief that his work would not come under the same scrutiny as it might have had a full 50 minutes been given to it. He attempted to retaliate silently in an 'I'll teach you attitude' by insisting that the ending time of the supervision was strictly observed. This same supervisor also did not have any regularity in the collection of fees, presenting bills as and when. The final fee due to the supervisor was never paid. The supervisee found, in a worried way, that he began to hold the supervisor in contempt. The theft in this case is obvious. Fortunately for the trainee and his future patients his other training supervisor and training therapist kept good boundaries thus ensuring that he internalised a good model of practice mitigating to a degree the effect of what was stolen.

Psychodynamic supervision relies on the sharing of fantasy. The patient comes alive in supervision through the words of the supervisee (see Chapter 1). The supervisor plays a role in the internal life of the supervisee and patient, extending the drama from two to three people. While it is generally accepted that therapists and patients strictly limit any contact outside of the therapy, boundaries between supervisors and supervisees are less well defined. While this may be inevitable, the shared fantasy of the patients' material is probably enhanced if there is as little contact as possible. There is then a need for supervisors and supervisees to strictly limit contact outside the supervision sessions and to be relatively anonymous to each other, for supervision, like therapy, affects our inner worlds and alters our inner objects. Theft of fantasy may occur if the supervisor over concretises the supervisory process by, for instance not using the information accessed through the reflection process. Theft of fantasy may also occur if the supervisor 'acts out' or 'in', in an anxious fashion. This may result in not determining the source of the anxiety, the supervisor's or the patient's reflected through the supervisee, and in essence ignoring the difference between therapy and supervision, between a dyadic and triadic activity. The sort of action which may result from this lack of knowledge might be becoming actively involved and attempting to influence or interfere directly in the work of therapy. Positively inviting telephone contact outside of the supervisory hour, giving the impression that the supervisor is there to sort out crises or to reassure the supervisee is to offer a model which is not congruent to therapy and which will not provide a useful container.

An example of the theft of fantasy is the following account of the supervision of a male patient who was in therapy with an experienced male supervisee.

The patient came from a large family. The father seemed to be successful but weak, the mother downtrodden but strong, much of her strength coming from deep religious convictions. The patient, a well-qualified professional, reported that as a child he had tried to earn his mother's love by forgoing play to join with her in her religious practices and to earn his father's love by becoming very competitive with his male siblings.

The patient presented with marked sadistic fantasies about women that he disguised with superficial over-concern for them. He would, for instance, literally give a 'helping hand' to an attractive woman who unwittingly took part in his sadistic fantasies by allowing him to touch her. While aggressive sexual language became commonplace in the therapy the language of love or tenderness was marked by its absence. The supervisee took the case for supervision to a female supervisor who in every session focused only on the detail of the supervisee/patient interactions and interpretations. The supervisee gradually discovered that on leaving most supervision sessions he felt dirty and that he had not done his 'homework' properly. It was as though he and the patient were not engaged in therapy but in a thrice-weekly homoerotic conversation that focused in a part object way on women. Fantasies of pin up calendars, or of teenage boys eyeing-up and talking about which 'girl is most likely to' came to mind. Presenting the work in supervision, the supervisee sensed that he was being censored continuously by the supervisor for allowing this situation to continue and not to get the patient to act in a way that would be more acceptable to his supervisor. This would probably reflect the patient's mother's wish for the patient to be a 'nice young man'. The supervisee experienced the supervisor as severe and therefore could not engage with her counter-transference feelings of dirtiness because it seemed that she was unable to engage with her unconscious to enable her to understand her own part in the triangular process.

There was much in the supervision which was a reflection of the patient's childhood, adolescent and present difficulties. Perhaps the supervisee was unconsciously projecting the religiously scrupulous mother onto the supervisor. The homoerotic aspect of the work was not commented on either, again the supervisor apparently acting out rather than interpreting through the reflection process the part of the religious mother. In a similar fashion to the patient's own early memories of his childhood the supervision was less than creative play, the supervisor keeping strictly to the verbatim, apparently not noticing the unconscious communication between the supervisor, the supervisee and the patient. The inability of the supervisor to give by use of her counter-transference meant that unconsciously she would not allow the supervisee to touch her. This and not using the reflection process caused the supervision and probably the therapy to be markedly impoverished.

Rutter's polemic (1990) was written out of outrage at his own psychotherapist's (and mentor's) sexual entanglement with a female patient. His observation was that sexual entanglements occur not just between obviously disturbed men and their patients but by accomplished professionals whose integrity was taken for granted. Rutter suggested that sexual violation of trust is a mainstream problem that re-enacts in a professional relationship a wider cultural power imbalance between men and women. However while the reporting of the sexualising of an erotic transference usually concerns heterosexual sex, supervisors also need to be aware of the possibility of homoerotic transference relationships becoming sexualised or of a 'Mrs Robinson' dynamic being created. The erotic transference and counter-transference often present therapeutic difficulties. Supervision therefore relies heavily on the integrity and courage of supervisees discussing cases that concern, particularly where erotic material is encountered. Supervisors need to be alert and listen out for problems which may be presented in the form of hints or through the supervisor's own counter-transference. An example of this can be seen in the following account.

A supervisee who worked in an organisation in which part of his role was that of staff counsellor. Staff either self-referred themselves or were referred through a manager. He was telephoned by a female manager wanting to self refer. He had met her earlier when she sought his help over a difficulty she was having with another staff member. Having already met her, he recalled thinking that he did not find her attractive and felt she disliked him. He thought the therapy might be difficult because of this but that there was likely not to be any strong erotic transference. Because of these thoughts he decided to discuss the initial angry and tearful session with his supervisor. He was somewhat shocked when the supervisor suggested that a strong erotic transference had immediately established itself between the patient and himself of which he was apparently unaware. The supervisee had repressed this aspect of the session but the supervisor had successfully been made aware of it through his own supervisor's counter-transference and thus was able to make this factor conscious for the therapist.

The sexualising of a therapeutic relationship is a serious matter and usually deemed to be a serious offence against most codes of ethics. It is hard to determine with any accuracy how frequently it occurs. This offence is a theft of fantasy. Similarly a theft of fantasy may also occur if a supervisory relationship becomes sexualised. Anecdotally it is reported that there is more sexualising of supervisee/supervisor relationships than therapist/patient relationships possibly because the supervisory relationship is not so closely held in the transference as is the therapist/patient relationship. Its frequency is again difficult to ascertain with any accuracy. Supervision is a situation where the very nature of the work, the language used, together with the shared professional intimacy can turn into a sexually explosive mix. While acknowledging the regressive aspects of supervision perhaps, both parties need to be aware of (and therefore responsible for) the conduct of the supervision. Regardless of the consequences that a sexual enactment may have between supervisor and supervisee, the sexualising of a supervisory relationship will have serious consequences for the patient at least at an unconscious level. Thus Gertrud Mander (Chapter 10) advocates that supervisors should themselves have supervisory support where transference issues between them and their supervisees can be discussed.

A frequently used aphorism of supervision is that it is 'more than teaching, less than therapy'. Theft of fantasy will occur if the material brought to supervision is used predominantly as clinical teaching material in the supervision, keeping the patient 'out there', treating the patient like a lump of pathology that is there to be learnt about and treated. Supervision is more than teaching because it has to incorporate the three participants into the inner world drama of the patient, acting more like a producer or arranger of the patient's set pieces.

Offences against the codes of ethics for supervisors, unlike their therapeutic equivalents, do not usually directly discredit the profession. Anecdotal tales of poor or unethical supervision tend to involve trainees and seem rarely to get officially reported. However minor the infringement, offences against a code of ethics or against the spirit of a code of ethics do constitute important frame modifications (Langs, 1994) and therefore will always have consequences in the therapy being supervised. There are many grey areas that probably give rise to anxiety from the over scrupulous and are misused by the under scrupulous. Murdin and Clarkson write that while the codes of ethics 'work well for the majority of supervisory relationships most of the time, sooner or later everyone comes across a conflict or an ambivalence where the code is not sufficient guidance' (1998: 107). Confidentiality is one such grey area.

The illusion of confidentiality – a conflict without resolution.

All who have shared the privilege of a personal analysis or therapy will understand how important trust is. This trust can be blind, patients placing their faith in the integrity of the therapist or of the reputation of the therapist's accrediting organisation. One aspect of such trust may be a belief that the therapist will not communicate to third parties details of their patients' personal, private and intimate fantasies. What about supervision?

Some therapists will make the subject of confidentiality conscious by making a statement about it at the initial meeting with a patient. Others may say nothing leaving the issue to evolve or not as part of the transference relationship. Both methods have their dangers. A statement of confidentiality may be vital to enable some patients to make full use of the therapy, others might be most helped by it not being mentioned.

So what is the value of either making a statement about confidentiality or by remaining silent on the matter. How important is it in the therapeutic setting? Immediately a case is presented for supervision, confidentiality between therapist and patient is breached and an ethical conflict is created. It does not matter that the supervisor or supervision group commit themselves to keeping the case material confidential, the mere fact of talking about a patient to colleague(s) creates the ethical conflict to which there is no easy solution. For instance attempting to enhance confidentiality by disguising the identity of the patient when presenting them for supervision merely adds to the difficulties (see Chapter 1). Liking supervision to a mother sharing her anxieties about her baby with her partner may be no more than an attempt at comforting rationalisation. Knowledge that the intimate conversations with a therapist may be reported to anonymous third parties for supervision will unconsciously affect the material presented by the patient.

Paradoxically if cases were not presented for supervision learning and development would be impeded. Additionally if cases were not presented for supervision, there would be less possibility of reassuring the public that the profession is adequately regulated. On the one hand, therapists are committed to confidentiality; on the other hand, they are committed to supervision. How is this apparent breach of confidentiality to be addressed in the therapy?

Some therapists will make the fact that they are in supervision conscious for the patient by referring to it in the initial meeting. The patient may enquire further or merely acknowledge this and make no further comment about it. Others will choose not to make this conscious by making no reference to their being in supervision part of the initial meeting, believing that as no explicit permission is required for them to present the work for supervision it is therefore of no concern of the patient. The patient may well not make any reference to it either during the initial interview or during the whole of the therapy. It is highly likely however, given how much common knowledge there now is about how therapy is organised, that a patient will be aware of supervision issues even if they have repressed such knowledge.

Some patients may make the subject of the therapist's supervision explicit themselves in the initial interview, perhaps to help them contain their anxiety or perhaps to check out the bona fides of the therapist. Others might want the therapist to be more explicit about what 'discussing it in supervision' means. Occasionally patients might specifically state that they do not wish the material to leave the consulting room (creating an ethical and management issue of its own).

Discussing work in supervision may stimulate new thoughts, angles and concepts about the work and the supervisee may experience an urge to share these with a larger audience. Thus supervision may itself promote further ethical conflicts between a duty to the patient to maintain confidentiality and a duty to the profession to advance knowledge by bringing clinical and theoretical hypotheses for case presentations or for publishing. Thus this chapter, while keeping to professional ethical guidelines breaches strict confidentiality.

The publication of Freud's case histories evidences that 'breaching (of) the confessional' (Bollas and Sundelson, 1995) occurred early in the profession's history. Scanning the collected works for Freud's or Jung's thoughts on patient confidentiality does not yield a very rich harvest. There is Freud's pragmatism:

> Certain patients want their treatment to be kept secret, often because they have kept their neurosis secret; and I put no obstacle in their way. That in consequence the world hears nothing of some of the most successful cures, is, of course, a consideration that cannot be taken into account. It is obvious that a patient's decision in favour of secrecy already reveals a feature of his secret history. (Freud, 1913: 136)

There is the linking of therapy with the ancient ritual of the Confessional, always a powerful symbol for Jung. 'Nothing makes people more lonely and more cut off from the fellowship of others, than the possession of an anxiously hidden and jealously guarded personal secret . . . here confession has a truly redeeming effect' (1961: 192).

In the earliest years of the psychoanalytic method, abreaction alone with its links to catharsis or cleansing, was thought to 'depotentiate the affectivity of a traumatic experience until it no longer has a disturbing influence' (Jung, 1954: 262). However Chapter 1 refers to Jung also using the word 'confession' in connection with supervision which suggests that Jung saw a parallel between therapy and supervision. In therapy, the patient confesses to the therapist, in supervision the therapist to the supervisor. Thus in his later years Jung wrote:

> Every therapist ought to have a control by some third person, so that he remains open to another point of view. Even the Pope has a confessor. I always advise analysts: 'Have a father confessor or a mother confessor!' Women are particularly gifted for playing such a part. They often have excellent intuition and a trenchant critical insight and can see what men have up their sleeves, at times see also into men's intrigues. They see aspects the man does not see. That is why no woman has ever been convinced her husband is a superman. (1963: 156)

It is likely that the emotional source for Jung's use of the word 'confession' was his early work with Sabina Spielrein (see Kerr, 1994) and in his need to seek help in this case he 'confessed' to Freud. Spielrein's conversations with Jung were of great intimacy. Therapeutic conversations are often likened to the conversations between mother and baby but they can also be likened to the conversation between lovers. Both use a language that signifies trust and dependency, which, if breached will cause great distress.

In 1982, Henderson, an American analyst published an account which clearly illustrates the dilemma of confidentiality and supervision. He tells of the supervision of a student psychotherapist who did not tell his patient that he was discussing him with Henderson in supervision. Sometime later, the patient was present at a public event at which Henderson, the supervisor, gave a paper. After the presentation Henderson reported that the patient exclaimed of him 'Who is that man? I must know him!' making clear that an unconscious form of recognition had been awakened in him during the presentation. He recognised Henderson only through the ideas communicated from Henderson through his supervisee, the patient's therapist. As Henderson pointed out, the exclamation should have been put the other way round – not 'I must know him!' but 'he must know me!'

It is hard to know let alone measure the actual effect on the outcome of the therapy when knowledge that whatever is talked about in therapy is likely to be passed on to a supervisor, even when the patient knows about it and has given tacit permission. The following example might offer some clues.

A markedly narcissistic male patient entered therapy with a male therapist who made no reference to supervision during the initial interview at which the contract was set up. The therapist was somewhat surprised when, at the end of the first session, the patient said 'that will keep your supervisor happy!' Similar remarks were repeated at the end of most of the early sessions. The therapist experienced these remarks as contemptuous and therefore tended to make interpretations along these lines. The therapist's experience of these remarks seemed confirmed when, after about six sessions, the patient brought a dream, which he contemptuously challenged the therapist to 'sort out'. The therapist was very aware of the enormous pressure to accept the challenge, to perform, to work it out, and carefully considered this along with his interpretation. The dream material centred on whether the patient could afford to accept the richness of what the therapist had to offer. After the interpretation and discussion in the session the patient dramatically changed his closing remark from 'this will keep your supervisor happy' to 'this will make a good paper for you to write when I've finished!' While the patient was someone who always seemed to be being invaded, whose life seemed to lack privacy where all seemed exaggeration, gossip and lies, there was a very deep secret which, perhaps because of shame or fear, was never discussed in therapy. It was only after his death, long after the therapy had ended, that, by chance, the therapist discovered what the secret was. It was that he knew he was HIV positive during the whole of the therapy, later dying of an AIDS related illness. The therapist realised that he never took this piece of work to supervision. The possible effect of his doing this was not about keeping confidentiality strictly, but about colluding with his patient's need to keep his secret, a secret. Had the therapist taken the work to supervision alternative ways of understanding the patient's remarks might have been opened out. This case highlights the paradox of confidentiality. On the one hand the patient might have been inhibited from sharing his nightmare fears with his therapist because of his fantasy of wanting to be the centre of attention of the supervisory discussion but fearing what this might entail. On the other the patient might have been inhibited to tell his secret because he unconsciously knew that the therapist was not discussing the work in supervision and, in fantasy, he might have feared that the therapist, not protecting himself with supervision would become prone to being psychically infected himself.

All who give or receive supervision will have experienced the apparent change that takes place in the therapy after a supervision session. The supervisor may have thrown new light, offering a new way of understanding the patient's material. Working closely together a peer supervision group, using their counter-transference, may have enabled a therapist to free up the entanglement he has had with the patient's internal world. The therapist will therefore feel freer when he next meets this patient. Often patients will let therapists know that something has changed, a change that raises issues for them. What has caused the change, the different emphasis, approach, direction? What has got into my therapist, how and why? How this is interpreted and understood is crucial, but at base line it is likely that unconsciously the patient knows that confidentiality has been breached.

Is it just a patient's pathology that makes them want to keep painful, embarrassing or personal material confidential? The problem of confidentiality is not a new phenomenon. The early church wrestled with the problem. Originally confessions were made in a group setting, but because of concern about the issue of confidentiality, over time group confessions became individual. Later the confessional box with its grilles constituted a further attempt to ensure anonymity. The confidentiality of the confessional was more or less enshrined in law – it only could be breached if national security was at stake.

There is no such legislation to protect therapists and while it can be persuasively argued that without supervision no training of therapists could take place; the argument that trained therapists need supervision to ensure that the interests of their patients are being met is less easily sustained. The supervision of trained therapists is not just concerned with overseeing their work as they, rather than the supervisor, choose what work to present for supervision. It follows therefore that no amount of supervision actually prevents therapists abusing their clients. As Gertrud Mander (1998) suggests, supervision gives abusive therapists the opportunity to abuse their supervisors as well as their patients.

This chapter is written in a time when the power of the confessional has been marginalised and in a milieu far removed from that of Jung and Freud. In modern society personal information is now routinely accessed by anonymous third parties for their own ends. Where one shops and for what, what one's taste is in music, the proportion of one's income spent on any group of items is revealed to anyone prepared to pay the price, and for some, certain information is priceless. CCTV cameras monitor our movements in city centres. We are told that this is 'for your security'. Except that as these films have been known to have been passed on to others for use as entertainment, the 'for your security' tag rings hollow. At what price security? The rationalisation that 'if you haven't anything to hide you won't mind' is used to justify most of these incursions into individual freedoms. This seems to echo Freud's idea that it is pathological to want privacy. At the moment anonymous man and anonymous woman, the great unseen, seem to tacitly agree to being routinely monitored. Perhaps like the majority of patients they expect to remain anonymous. This may go some way to account for the way the indiscretions of those who are in the public eye and therefore known are received and treated.

It is in this milieu that Bollas and Sundelson's notion that '. . . confidentiality is timeless . . . no person seeking an analysis should *ever* have his or her identity published without permission' (1995: 184) was conceived. At what price confidentiality? Bollas and Sundelson, while making no comment about whether confidentiality included presenting patient material in supervision, suggest that 'ever' means for the life of the therapist and beyond. Langs's (1994) excellent suggestions for securing the frame of supervision avoids the inherent conflict as well. While he suggests that all efforts are to be made by supervisor and supervisee to ensure the privacy of the patient's material, he seems not to recognise that the act of discussing a patient in supervision is, in essence, frame deviant.

Bollas and Sundelson make no reference to Freud or to any of the psychoanalytic pioneers in their book, supporting their contention that confidentiality ('as old as the Hippocratic Oath' (1995: 5)) has surprisingly little reasoned support in the profession. They argue for clarity and honesty concerning the subject of confidentiality at the commencement of treatment. They argue for the profession to be alive to the uniqueness of the therapeutic situation where one person might be allowed to explore with another their darkest fears and fantasies. Supervisors therefore always need to be alive to the manner in which their supervision is affecting the therapy. In other words supervisors need to keep constantly in the forefront of their minds the question of how the last session had been received by the supervisee, communicated to the patient and how that is being reported back to them.

Perhaps total confidentiality remains a dangerous illusion. For confidentiality frequently metamorphosises into secrecy, and secrecy can feel abusive, and often is abusive. Supervisors, therefore, have to tread an ethical tightrope between control and release to enable the patients to maintain whatever illusion of confidentiality is necessary for them to make the fullest use of the therapy and at the same time enable appropriate control to be exerted. Psychoanalytic therapy has been called 'A most dangerous method' (Kerr, 1994). Supervision is required to enable therapists to live dangerously, to control creativity creatively, and to ensure what is made public to them is kept private.

A Note on the Data Protection Act

Supervisees' notes contain their thoughts, responses, ideas, fantasies as well as more objective comments about patients. Supervisors' notes have a similar content. Such notes are often shorthand coded, personal and intended for self reflection and not communication to third parties. They represent information that has been thought to be confidential to the writer alone. The Data Protection Act is intended to ensure that information regarded as confidential is not in effect a secret which is kept from the subjects possibly to be used detrimentally against them. Such acts are attempts to ensure that this information can no longer remain hidden, and as such are to be welcomed. What effect the Data Protection Act has on therapists' and supervisors' note taking and keeping is beyond the scope of this chapter. An article, which the author considers to be clear and helpful, was published by BACP in its journal *Counselling*, 12(2): 109. Another useful article is a case study written from an agency manager's perspective on an attempt to use therapists' note taking as legal evidence. It was included in the BAPPS members' newsletter published in February 2000.

Note

The British Association for Counselling and Psychotherapy publishes a monthly journal *Counselling* and can be contacted at 1 Regent Place, Rugby, Warwickshire CV21 2PJ.

The British Association for Psychoanalytic and Psychodynamic Supervision can be contacted either at bapad@wadbapps.freeserve.co.uk or at PO BOX 419, Redhill, Surrey RH9 8DL.

References

Barnett, R. (2001) 'Therapy Session Notes: Changes in Law and Practice', *BAPPS Newsletter*, 6(1).

Bollas, C. and Sundelson, D. (1995) *The New Infomants*. London: Karnac Books.

Cassell (1979) *Cassell's English Dictionary*. London: Cassell.

Freud, S. (1913) *On Beginning the Treatment*, Standard Edition, 12. London: Hogath Press.

Henderson, J. (1982) 'Assessing progress in supervision' *Journal of Analytical Psychology*, 27(105): 130.

Jung, C.G. (1954) 'Problems of Modern Psychotherapy', in *Collected Works 16*, The Practice of Psychotherapy. London: Routledge. pp. 53–75.

Jung, C.G. (1961) 'Freud and Psychoanalysis' in *Collected Works 4*. London: Routledge.

Jung, C.G. (1963) 'Psychiatric activities', in *Memories Dreams, Reflections*. London: Routledge. pp. 135–168.

Kerr, J. (1994) *A Most Dangerous Method*. London: Sinclair Stevenson.

Langs, R. (1994) *Doing Supervision and Being Supervised*. London: Karnac Books.

Mander G. (1998) 'Dyads and triads: some thoughts on the nature of therapy supervision', in P. Clarkson (ed.) *Supervision, Psychoanalytic and Jungian Perspectives*. London: Whurr Publishers. pp. 53–63.

Murdin, L. and Clarkson, P. (1998) 'The ethical dimensions of supervison' in P. Clarkson (ed.) *Supervision, Psychoanalytic and Jungian Perspectives*. London: Whurr Publishers. pp. 107–121.

Rutter, P. (1990) *Sex in the Forbidden Zone*. London: Unwin.

Chapter 10

Supervision of Supervision: Specialism or New Profession?

Gertrud Mander

In the BACP Code of Ethics and Practice for Supervisors of Counsellors (1996) the supervision of supervision work is listed (A.6. Competence) as a necessary part of the supervisor's ongoing monitoring and developing of his or her own competence. It therefore looks as if in future it might become mandatory to have regular consultations on one's supervision work and, as a consequence of this requirement, there will be a whole new dimension to supervision which has developed naturally in the course of people being trained in supervision. It seems at first a bit like the old chestnut about the hierarchy among fleas, or like Parkinson's Law – growth for growth's sake. We need to be careful what we are doing about this in order to stop an unnecessary and unwieldy proliferation of watchdogs *ad infinitum*. On the other hand, the problems and dilemmas of doing supervision are no less than the problems and dilemmas of doing therapy, and the belief in supervision goes hand in hand with the notion that everybody's work benefits from being regularly thought about and shared with another practitioner.

Over the years of training supervisors (including being trained as a supervisor myself) I have taken for granted the task of supervising supervision, much as the previous generation of supervisors took it for granted that they could do the job of supervision because they had once been supervised and were experienced therapists. But now I feel the time has come to start thinking systematically about what I was doing in the small supervision groups on the supervision training that I organised and in the consultations I am occasionally asked to do for experienced supervisors. In what way is supervising supervision the same and in what way is it different from the supervision of therapeutic work?

One could start to think of it as the next rung of a ladder (not a hierarchy) indicating a further distance from the bottom rung where the client/patient is located and hence further away from their projections, pain and chaos that ensnare the therapist and perplex the supervisor: in other words, as gaining a loftier view and a better space for thinking. Or one can see it as the expansion of a hall of mirrors, and hence as a multiplication of the reflections and refractions caused for the participants in the supervision by the anxieties and the defences against those operating in the supervisory and in the therapeutic field. But both metaphors have their limitations, as they merely denote a spatial difference, the addition of another dimension, without explaining the function or the benefit of the exercise, which is to help supervisors manage and understand their supervision work and to stop them from getting into trouble.

Plainly speaking, there are more persons and relationships to be considered and contained: four people and three relationships, in fact, which form a whole network of groupings and sub-groups. This means a need for even greater flexibility and objectivity on the part of the supervisor's supervisor, or metaphorically, for an even wider-angle lens to take in a bigger field, for a subtle camera mind which takes in flashbacks, close-ups, stills, processes and patterns, and homes in quickly and intuitively on the problem area flagged up by the presenter. Moving between client, supervisee and supervisor is possible only if the clinical material has been pre-processed and pre-focused by the presenter in such a way that the consultant can get to work on it without having to wade through a thicket of unnecessary detail. Concision and close attention are of the essence: by pinpointing the supervisor's counter-transference issues, anxieties and defenses the consultant will narrow down the field to a particular focus on an achievable target.

In my experience, finding the target is often a difficulty when a supervisee is resisting, in one of the many unconscious ways resistance manifests itself in supervision, or when there is a narcissistic concern for one or the other of the participants, in particular the client. In other words, the problem is likely to be a regressive transference situation that has eluded the therapist and that now reverberates in the whole supervisory field, with the supervisor also unable to understand or to resolve it. The supervisor's supervisor will be called upon to attend to a knotty problem in either the therapeutic or the supervisory couple that has so far defeated attempts at interpreting the reflection processes. Many a gridlocked supervision situation could be avoided if it were taken to supervision before becoming intractable, obstructing the supervisee's learning and stopping creative clinical work.

This applies equally to training situations as to work with experienced therapists or supervisors, in organisations and in private practice, and it presupposes the willingness to declare work problems, mistakes and dilemmas openly and honestly. The former is usually an agreed assessment situation and the task is tied to a stated goal – the award of a diploma or of accreditation in supervision – where the supervisor has the power to make or break the trainee's career. The latter involves the voluntary opening of one's professional books in order to get another mind to work on situations beyond one's understanding or problem-solving abilities and to shed more light on a difficult matter, to think the unthinkable in the company of another. Both situations require much ego strength and a reasonably strong sense of self, otherwise the fear of being shamed and humiliated may lead to resistance and to an unconscious sabotaging of the task.

In training situations there is a tendency to blame the trainee for difficulties arising in supervision which impede their learning. Ekstein and Wallerstein (1958), in their book *The Teaching and Learning of Psychotherapy* listed only the trainee therapist's learning problems. The psychoanalyst Barbara Stimmel, (1995) is the first to turn the spotlight on the supervisor's denied feelings and on the danger of defensively using reflective process monitoring. Thus the supervisor's supervisor has the task of monitoring and uncovering this defensiveness, to look as carefully at the supervisor's narcissism, projections and transferences (both positive and negative) as at the supervisee's. I have noticed that supervisors with a didactive, confrontational or authoritarian style which can be a theoretical dogmatism or a function of being in a powerful training role, tend to produce rebelliousness and stubbornness in trainees, and that then the supervisee's refusal to do what they are told may lead to a vicious circle, preventing all learning and relating (including the client's). On the other hand, as Stimmel demonstrates, the supervisor who denies their loving feelings, will tend towards favouritism which can undermine objectiveness and allow the trainee/supervisee too much free rein – in the spirit of 'do what you want'. Support turns into permissiveness and containment into licence. Sailing between the Scylla of authoritarianism and the Charybdis of permissiveness is the dangerous and difficult craft of supervision, and the supervisor's supervisor has the responsible task of ensuring a safe passage, of navigating the inexperienced and when the worst comes to the worst, of rescuing the shipwrecked. This can go as far as a complaint or an appeal, or it may simply mean a careful separation of the protagonists, including the supervisee's terminating their training or clientwork. As there are always clients involved in this scenario, it is necessary to act swiftly for their sake.

Compared to plain supervision, there is a decisive difference in the supervisor–supervisor relationship that is a difference due to the levels of experience and expertise to be found in both partners in the relationship. In this instance, both participants in the exercise are practising the same craft (in contrast to plain supervision and therapy where one participant expects the other to have knowledge of how the task is to be done) and this allows them, on the one hand, to use professional shorthand, but on the other hand their unconscious competitive and envious impulses may be activated in pursuit of the task. It is up to the supervisor's supervisor to monitor the levels of this latter phenomenon and to name them when it becomes necessary and fruitful to the clinical work as it may turn out to be a reflection from the therapeutic relationship. Then its exploration will open up the competitive issue naturally, or it may originate in one of the two supervisory relationships when the frank revealing and owning of it can stop it from rippling back into the therapy in an unhelpful way. All this requires what in German is called *fingerspitzengefühl*, i.e., tact and firmness and authoritativeness on the part of the supervisor's supervisor. But what if it doesn't work? Will the supervisor's supervisor then need consultations with a supervisor of supervision of supervision? The mind boggles at so much complexity and the likelihood of a problem getting passed on up an endless ladder (Rioch, 1980).

On the other hand, the colleagueship scenario in which mentorship rather than tutorial or parental attitudes prevail, allows for creative joint thinking about practicalities like contracts, frames, functions, characteristic dilemmas, for the frank voicing of doubts and hypotheses, the questioning of fundamentals, and the trying out of new theories. I find myself comparing notes with supervisors more frankly and frequently than as a therapist's supervisor, picking someone else's brains, enjoying disagreements or arguments, in the sportive spirit of pitting oneself against a protagonist of roughly equal strength, and when the chips are down, agreeing to disagree in a Socratic spirit of 'what do we really know?'

When it is done in a group, the supervision of supervision can be very stimulating and satisfying because everyody can play the game, can co-supervise and contribute to the pool of insights equally and creatively. Yet it can also become quite explosive when there are fundamental differences of opinion due to hidden agendas, to dogmatic rigidities or to sibling rivalries, and then the group supervisor is called upon to manage and contain the emotional intensities as they can severely limit and obsruct the creative interplay of ideas. In one group, for instance, I had a male supervisor who focused on Oedipal issues, homeostasis, Eros and Thanatos, in confrontation with a female supervisor who always homed in on primitive psychotic processes and demanded that these be worked on first. I usually saw it coming when they got close to a fight over how to explore a case and I always aimed to name conflicts before they could turn into acrimonious confrontations. That way there was an acknowledgment of creative difference, of the many ways to the truth and of a toleration of pluralistic solutions. It became possible to turn to the man for an Oedipal hypothesis and to the woman for a formulation of the narcissistic disturbance, and the group managed to function without threatening to break apart, though there were always scary moments before the diffusion of conflict.

As in plain supervision I always spend some time finding out the particularities of a supervisor's style of processing material and observe their inimitable ways of associating, thinking, relating and structuring (Jacobs et al., 1995). Strengths and weaknesses will soon become apparent, and so will each individual's management of anxiety – in the forementioned case the man took over the group and became didactic and verbose in defence of his anxiety, while the woman became aloof and intellectual, worried about the client's disturbance levels and containment needs and about the therapist's inexperience of psychotic processes. The third trainee supervisor, a group therapist, sat quietly observing, keeping her head down and leaving the dynamic interpreting to me. Almost every session in that group was a dramatic happening, but then perhaps every supervision session should be some kind of happening or revelation – as learning happens on a largely unconscious level, it cannot be fashioned or produced consciously, only facilitated or set in motion. This is why talking at people in a didactic way is so chancy and unpredictable in its outcome, as it depends on the quality of listening and hearing in which it is received.

Allowing for difference in thinking styles and anxiety management is the secret of good supervision of supervision. Obviously, I try to beware of offering my solutions when the toleration of not understanding is more apposite and when a situation needs to develop further before it becomes clear to the supervisor or supervisee what is going on in the supervision under scrutiny. I often think of Winnicott's squiggles, his doodling with the baby, and remind myself that all that needs doing usually is to push the matter slightly forward – with a question, a suggestion, a quote from another supervision situation, or with a story of one's own difficulties in learning.

The big temptation for the supervisor of supervision, as in therapy and plain supervision, is to be knowing and all-knowing (Gee, 1996). The unsolved problem, the overriding anxiety and the distress of not knowing make a strong appeal to one's omnipotence implying that one magic word, one idea or one piece of advice may do the trick. Also, the supervisor or supervisor's supervisor is usually very relieved when, after an initial period of uncertainty while he or she tries to take in and understand what the supervisee is talking about, there is a flash of insight as to what the problem might be or what might be needed, followed by the irresistible urge to play this back at once to the supervisee: 'I think I know and can offer you a solution'. Instead of which the holding on to the insight, the facilitating of the supervisee's understanding and thinking around the problem, and the further opening up of the material will almost always lead to a combining of forces and hopefully to the joint free-associating and thinking that equips for further action.

The narcissistic pleasure of being the one in the know is difficult to curb, but in my experience it is ultimately less satisfying (because it is also guilt-inducing) than being present when the other person in the session makes a discovery, comes to an understanding or makes a connection. 'What I know, I only know for myself', said Goethe which would mean in this context that for my meaning to become the supervisee's meaning it needs to be transformed into a spark that ignites in his or her mind. In other words, my connection makes a projective leap – which is often called inspiration: an unconscious, spiritual means of communicating. What is necessary is the ability to wait, to believe and to trust in the supervisee's ability eventually to deal with the situation and to find their own way through the maze of clinical material. The simple truth is: when they feel trusted, they can trust themselves.

Of course, there are always subsidiary needs, in particular those for support and praise. I have become aware, as supervisee and as supervisor, that it is essential for supervision to be a space where good work can be taken and will be received. This is the mirroring function of supervision. The supervisee indicates, I am excited about that session when something amazing happened and I must tell you about it. Or, I am pleased with myself for having contained that aggressive outburst and interpreted this particular defensive system, please, take note and give me your approval. I think this side of the joint work can be neglected in the attempt to identify problems and dilemmas, or to expect rapid development and change, in client, supervisee, and supervisor. There is a strong element of nurturing to supervision, and to the supervision of supervision, that relates to the provision of a facilitating environment, to the holding function that underpins the thinking function and enables the confronting, probing, uncovering endeavour that is the most painstaking aspect of all supervision work.

What I find I need as a supervisor (of therapists and of supervisors) is the supervisee's trust and their adaptation to my request to be presented with the material in a form I can work with. Apart from the strict verbatim, which is essential in the training situation, people's presentations vary enormously and depend on the degree of articulacy and fluency of the individual, as well as to their ability to organise and process a mass of details. As I am myself a fairly diffident talker, preferring listening to talking, and writing to talking off the cuff, I never tire of listening to the different narratives I am presented with in the course of a full working week, and feel privileged to be let in on so many human difficulties and dilemmas. But while some presenters allow me to get hold of a situation almost immediately, others can lead me astray or cause me confusion which will require much clarification and cross-questioning before my own organising and processing can come into play. How much that owes to the client can only be decided in each individual case.

This is particularly evident when it is a one-off situation, a consultation or an unfamiliar case. We all have the experience of supervisees who swamp us with narrative detail of the 'I said, he said' type in which one promptly drowns. There are others who wrap the clinical detail into layers of conjecture and speculation based on their articles of faith. Others again merely hand you a jumble of facts to work on or a discrete piece of interaction without setting it into its context. Some presenters turn into brilliant performers delivering star turns in which wit and charm transform the content of an ordinary counselling session into a dramatic dialogue apparently informed by total recall – complete with running commentary on the psychodynamics of the interaction. I remember one particular supervisee who had perfected that art of virtuoso presenting to a point where I was unable to tell fact from fiction – and almost lost my own powers of reflection in the process. The aim, of course, was to impress and be admired. The narcissistic presenter is a seducer – away from or into his or her case, at a heavy cost in terms of truth and shareability. The supervisor is turned into a captive audience and made redundant, depotentiated. Most common and most irritating of all for me, however, is the supervisee who brings a case and says with sublime innocence 'you will remember such-and-such'. Or 'you told me to do this and that' expecting my memory instantly to retrieve all the facts I was told weeks or months before, as if from a divinely functioning computer filing system. I usually say, please fill me in or remind me. When it is an ongoing situation, I ask for a written profile or a thumbnail sketch which I can refer to while the current clinical material is presented. It is surprising how quickly one's memory throws up the relevant detail associatively or how a minimum of information can lead into a depth of exploration.

I have not yet addressed the particular psychodynamic dimension of the supervision of supervision, and the importance of foursomes or mandalas.

To start with the latter: there is a symmetry to the supervision of supervision, in contrast to the asymmetry of plain supervision, where in Mattinson's (1975) by now classic formulation Oedipal dimensions like inclusion and exclusion predominate. Here the supervisory couple balances the therapeutic couple and, as in Ekstein and Wallerstein's (1958) clinical rhombus, a four-cornered scenario comes about in which the lines of communication are manifold and complex. The physical action happens in three rooms, one of which remains outside the experience of both supervisors, and they have to imagine together what happens in it. Using their intuition, their counter-transference and other indicators pinpointing the unconscious communications in the multi-dimensional emotional field, they attempt to home in on the conflicts, anxieties and defences against these which cause the supervisory presenting problem. It always seems like a small miracle to me that, by intuition or luck we manage to focus on something significant that leads to the unravelling of an intractable or knotty situation, a stuckness pervading the whole field, a blind spot, something transferential or unthinkable.

For this miracle to happen everything depends on the swift concentrating and condensing of the interactions and actions occurring simultaneously on the various stages, within the four different visual fields of the mandala. It is an experience like looking at the picture of a landscape in which many things go on at the same time, as in Breughel's 'The Fall of Icarus' where the splash of Icarus's fall and of his struggling legs disappearing into the sea are positioned in the far right-hand corner while on shore a farmer is calmly ploughing his field and in the middle distance a splendid ship is sailing towrds a city on the shore. Breughel's famous painting can make a useful metaphor for supervision work. In the painting as so often in supervision, the eye is drawn away from ordinary dull detail to what is going on around it. Like the subjects in the painting, supervisors have to turn their back on the apparent richness of the tapestry and concentrate on the everyday material. So, whilst the supervisee's presentation often consists of such a broad painting, full of interesting narrative detail, it is the detail that needs to be carefully sifted, by using evenly hovering attention, for the meaningful nexus which Daniel Stern (1985) called the 'key therapeutic metaphor'. When this is found the supervisor can make a dynamic intervention and start a process of co-operative reflection on the essential features of the patient's clinical material and on the significant points in the supervisory field where transference and counter-transference issues provide possible answers to difficult questions posed by the supervisee.

Hinshelwood (1991) advises when doing assessment to search out the point of maximum pain; others talk of the core complex Glasser, (1993), the basic fault Balint (1968) or the core conflictual relationship Luborsky (1990) which underlie the complex picture. It is one of the fatal temptations of supervisors to go astray and away from the pain when they allow their passion for intellectual analysis to take over instead of focusing on the internal human drama which is hidden in the broad canvas. The picture of the fall of Icarus is, in this respect, a doubly felicitous choice – Icarus, whom his father Daedalus cannot restrain, was imprudently flying towards the sun and paid for this by being blinded and drowning. Being blinded and drowning can happen during supervision and also during the supervision of supervision; drowning in too much clinical material, in idle speculation, in hypothesising and analysing obsessively removed from the real action, the real dilemma, the real pain. Then one's own preoccupations, narcissistic needs, personal and theoretical assumptions will get in the way of what I have called the 'necessary happening' that makes supervision and the supervision of supervision meaningful and creative. The constant vigilance that Karl Popper (1962) advised citizens in democratic states to exercise towards their elected representatives, is as essential an attitude for supervisors to observe towards their charges and themselves.

I want to finish with the reminder that everything ultimately needs to be brought back to the client, and that we must always boldly embrace the whole ambit of the shifting focus, which moves from the client's story to the therapist's counter-transference to the supervisor's dilemma and finally starts something up in the mind of the supervisor of the supervision that can be used to make a creative and meaningful supervisory intervention.

References

BACP (1996) *Code of Ethics and Practice for Supervisors of Counsellors*. Rugby, Warwickshire: BACP.

Balint, M. (1968) *The Basic Fault*. London: Tavistock Publications.

Ekstein, R. and Wallerstein, R. (1958) *The Teaching and Learning of Psychotherapy*. Madison, CT: International Universities Press.

Gee, H. (1997) 'Developing insight through supervision: relating then defining', *Journal of Analytical Psychology*, 41(4): 529–552.

Glasser, M. (1993) 'Problems in the psychoanalysis of certain narcissistic disorders', *The International Journal of Psycho-Analysis*, 73(3).

Hinshelwood, R.D. (1991) 'Psychodynamic formulation for assessment in psychotherapy', *British Journal of Psychotherapy*, 8(2): 166–174.

Jacobs, D., David, P. and Meyer, D.J. (1995) *The Supervisory Encounter*. New Haven and London: Yale University Press.

Luborsky, L. and Crits-Christoph, P. (1990) *Understanding Transference: The CCRT Method*. New York: Basic Books.

Mattinson, J. (1975) *The Reflection Process in Casework Supervision*. London: The Institute of Marital Studies.

Popper, K. (1962) *The Open Society and its Enemies*. London: Routledge.

Rioch, M. (1980) 'The dilemmas of supervision in dynamic psychotherapy', in A.K. Hess (ed.), *Psychotherapy Supervision, Theory, Research and Practice*. New York: John Wiley & Sons.

Stern, D. (1985) *The Interpersonal World of the Infant*. New York: Basic Books.

Stimmel, B. (1995) 'Resistance to awareness of the supervisor's transferences with special reference to the parallel process', *International Journal of Psycho-Analysis*, 76: 609–618.

Chapter 11

Timing and Ending in Supervision

Gertrud Mander

I have chosen to think about the issues of timing and ending in supervision which are similar and yet different in many respects from counselling. Beyond technicalities to do with contexts and professional requirements there is the fact that more relationships are involved – the therapeutic, the supervisory and the three-person dynamic which is under constant observation in psychodynamic supervision. This means that a third person – the client – though physically absent in the supervision session needs to be considered in all matters of timing and ending and this factor alters and complicates the processes considerably and significantly, requiring a number of skills that supervisors need to learn and add to their therapeutic armamentarium.

Timing

In the first part of this chapter I shall be dividing the subject of timing in supervision into three parts.

First *time as horizontal*, i.e. the length and duration of supervisory contracts, when and why to change supervisors and when to stop, altogether or for the time it takes to find a replacement, to make a transition and to reorganise work. The question will be: can we ever be without supervision? Second, *time as vertical*: time and timing in the supervisory session, structuring, interventions, format and frame issues. Third, *the role of memory in supervision*. How do busy supervisors cope with the mass of material, persons, names, incidents, feelings and projections they are presented with and how does their memory store and retrieve information as necessary?

By taking the three sections one after the other, I hope to establish some idea of the multiplicity and complexity of time dimensions in supervision as it differs from therapy, with which it is always intertwined.

The horizontal dimension

In the course of one's working life as a therapist one encounters many embodiments of supervision. Sometimes and not unusually, one has simultaneous supervisors for different parts of one's workload: in an agency, in private practice, for one's long-term psychotherapy patients, for the short-term work done for an employment agency, for a hospital placement, clinic or GP surgery, and last but not least for one's own supervision work. This means adapting to different styles and personalities, to endings and beginnings which have not always been carefully prepared. Some of these situations are short-lived, not necessarily of one's own choosing, and are managerial in character in that they may vary in frequency and in the number of clients attended to. Others may extend over years of fruitful collaboration and then the role of the supervisor will resemble that of an athlete's coach in its influence on the supervisee's professional development, its intimate knowledge of the therapist's strengths and weaknesses, of the patients and the therapeutic relationships with them.

A supervisor can last as long or as short as a therapist, and the supervisory relationship undergoes similar permutations over its duration as the therapeutic relationship in terms of negative and positive feelings and transferences. However, the projections are usually less intense and on the whole there can be more equality, resistance and regression are two integral parts of the learning achieved in supervision. The anxieties and irksome responsibilities of preparation, of coming and going on time, of breaks and fees punctuate the regularity of meeting and working for the task, and only the exceptional supervisee does not baulk against the yoke of supervision with its concomitant experiences of exposure, self-doubt, confusion and depressing inadequacy.

Fortunately these experiences are offset by the times when supervision becomes a happening, a revelation of insights and truths impossible to gain on one's own, an affirmation of something done well, a togetherness of thinking and discovering that underlines the value of what we do. As long as we experience both, and hopefully more of the latter times, there is value in supervision and the supervisor is achieving their aim. When it becomes stale, monotonous, boring and repetitive it is time to leave, as the supervisee may have outgrown the supervisor, whose capacity to be creative may have become undermined by envy or fear of exposure. This is a notable difference in supervision from therapy as the levels of professional ability are always changing, and probably more rapidly, though not inevitably in the supervisee. The supervisor may simply have reached the limit of her capacity to absorb, digest and expand knowledge and understanding, with age, overload or increasing routine. This may be uttering a heresy in a world which believes in ongoing individuation, but I believe it needs examining.

The important question can be reframed: is there an optimal length for supervisory contracts and, more radically, is there ever a time to hand over the task to the internal supervisor and call it a day for paid supervision?

BACP says two years to the first part of the question and never to the second part, but this takes no account of the experienced practitioner and relates to the supervision of counsellors, who generally work once-weekly, have not had much personal therapy as a rule and need support and holding when clients become demanding and act out.

Changing the supervisor every two years is a prescriptive rule that is meant to curb collusion and encourage diversity of learning. It can, however, perpetuate the training situation in which supervision is prescribed to an extent that resistance becomes inevitable. Moreover, once out in the world of private work the therapist finds that therapeutic contracts lengthen and the same then happens with supervisory contracts. On the one hand, following individual cases carefully over the years requires ongoing supervisory relationships; on the other, it is surprising how much one's clinical work can benefit from a change of perspective. Thus instead of having to follow a rule it should be left to the individual to decide when to change supervisors, and in reality this is often dictated by external circumstances.

As for doing without supervision there cannot be a prescriptive rule either, though it is surely unethical and unprofessional to think that one might come to a point of total autonomy and professional wisdom. I also believe that the urge to share one's professional delights and dilemmas is irrepressible, and that it might lead us astray into gossip and boasting in informal situations if not bound into a more formal commitment. Finally the constant unconscious pressure of psychopathology should not be underestimated. Therapists become powerful people in their patients' lives and get seduced easily into omnipotence or grandiosity. Discussing ethics with my long-term supervisor taught me early on that it is not only the obvious temptations of sexual or financial gratification which are most dangerous but the possibility that the isolated therapist's narcissism increases and even that he or she might go mad. There is the likelihood too that the therapist ignores the warning signs of burn-out and underestimates the incapacity due to illness or old age. Our self-esteem is always bound up with our work. We feel important and often indispensable to our patients. Ideally a supervisor should be able to call a halt and exert authority when these issues arise. And as this is a profession where people do not have to retire when others are forced to, there should be some supervisory safeguard for everybody. But it cannot be prescribed, rather it should be recommended, and facilitated to enable therapists to monitor and decide for themselves.

I personally favour a compromise of occasional breaks in supervision, reduction of frequency, establishment of reading and discussion groups with peers, and with growing experience, a ready-made group of colleagues to consult with regularly or sporadically, leaving open the possibility of reverting to regular supervision whenever the clinical work demands new input or investigation of unexamined work practices. If there is no supervision, there are two absolute imperatives: that the therapist has a colleague whom s/he entrusts with her list of patients and supervisees while on holiday or for unforseeable emergencies and that s/he has an agreement with a colleague or colleagues to tell honestly when they are concerned about her suitability for continuing work. It is the ultimate test of good colleagueship to tell another that the time has come to let go, temporarily or for good.

Vertical time and timing in supervision

In contrast to the therapist, as a supervisor one is generally in charge of structuring and timekeeping the supervisory session, unless the model used is very analytical or person-centred. There are, however, many ways of using the time and involving the supervisee/s in the task, and the timing of supervisory interventions is one of the skills a supervisor needs to develop and monitor. However, what is natural for me may be anathema for someone else, and therefore I want to state a first obvious rule of thumb.

Supervisors are influenced by their own supervisors in that they either practise the way they experienced it or, if that was not a good experience, the way they would have liked to have been supervised. Unless, of course, they have been trained, and deliberately modified their 'natural' style in the course of their training.

Many years of supervising supervisors have taught me that supervisees also influence the supervisor's style, though not necessarily always for the better. I am talking about their resistance; their individual ways of receiving or not receiving supervisory input in relation to their therapeutic work. This further depends on where they are in their training or their practice: some want to be spoonfed, others insist on doing it all their own way, others again need constant approval or need to go into dramatic detail in order to present their therapeutic dilemmas, successes and failures.

Like the therapist, the supervisor needs to listen first to the personal voice and special appeal of the supervisee, to recognise their particular style of processing and thinking about clinical material, their idiosyncratic way of being with another – be it the patient or the supervisor – and then to adapt or fashion their responses accordingly. I do not mean that my ideal supervisor is a chameleon, rather, that we try to tune into the supervisory partner no less sensitively than mother to baby, friend to friend, or therapist to patient, while holding on to who we are and sticking firmly to the task which, in each supervisory session, has the goal of making something happen. Here is my second rule of thumb.

Supervision is about making something happen. This requires a number of ingredients. First, a good enough relationship in which difficulties can be aired without undue anxiety, shame, fictional embellishment or distortion. Then, a belief in the process of putting into words an experience with a patient – be it a whole session, the development of an interaction, or, most often, a transference event that allows a new reading of the patient's story or pathology – and the belief that this process will allow another mind to participate and reflect creatively on the many issues active in the therapeutic endeavour.

Further, the willingness to engage in a joint search for meaning and understanding that will result in the fruitful continuation of the therapist's activities of listening, interpreting, containing and reflecting on the patient's communicated material. This willingness involves taking verbal and emotional risks to do with intimacy, fear of failure and of exposure, envy, regression, misunderstanding or miscalculation. This applies to both partners in the exercise, and as there is always a third person involved, these risks involve experiences of inclusion and exclusion. The supervisee's possessiveness towards the patient may cause the supervisor concern for the patient, and this can turn into clumsy intrusiveness, know-all cleverness or into a mutative intervention that will illuminate something the therapeutic couple were unconscious of, and that will help them move on in their endeavour to understand the conflicts, anxieties and defences against them that cause the patient's suffering.

It is the latter happening that constitutes a good hour in supervision. How does the supervisor make it happen, or, rather, what indicates that such a happening has taken place?

As with Strachey's (1934) mutative interpretation, there are a number of conditions necessary for this felicitous event. First, in the supervisee, an allowance of unconscious regression and lowering of defences that produce spontaneous remembering, linking and insight. Second, an intuitive hunch in the supervisor that transforms factual information into creative hypothesis, that homes in perhaps on a re-enactment in the transference, or makes sense of a bizarre counter-transference experience related by the supervisee, all of which leads to the spotlight moving onto something the patient has communicated to the therapist. It often takes a long time to get to this in a case presentation, probably requiring much clarification of detail, some tentative linking of the client's primary relationships with the here and now of the therapeutic interaction, and the identification of something at first inexplicable and unusual that is going on in the supervisory couple.

My own practice and experience is somewhat like this: I listen to the presentation as attentively and openly as possible, in that state of unpreoccupied and intense receptiveness that Freud (1912) and Bion (1962) have best described. Keeping my options open until something strikes me I collect my stray thoughts and hypotheses as if in one part of my mind while with the other I try to form a picture of what the supervisee is telling me. There is always a long period of uncertainty when I haven't a clue, and when in my experience it is best not to come in with conjectures or conclusions no matter how eager the supervisee may be for an opinion or a reassuring concurrence with their reading of the material. When supervision happens in a group I let the group members have their say first and this usually leads me to the point that has escaped me so far. In individual supervision I may play for time by asking for more detail, eliciting bits to which the supervisee unconsciously has turned a blind eye. To facilitate this I may play devil's advocate, or play with the material by using analogies or comparisons with my own clinical and personal experience. Somehow finally the interaction with the supervisee throws up a thought that leads into the material and to a natural focus where the supervisee may have stopped in their tracks unable to go on with the meaning-making that allows helpful and well-timed interpretations.

Though supervision does not use interpretation the way it is used in therapy, the function of supervisory interventions – be it the offering of a hypothesis concerning the patient's psychopathology, the suggestion of a possible transference link, the naming of a defensive strategy, the questioning of a technical point, the introduction of some apposite theory – is to make something conscious that the supervisee is still groping for. This can be done in a facilitating sort of way, by asking 'what do you think is going on' or 'can you look at it in another way perhaps?' Or, more didactically, by conceptualising the situation with the help of some theory, and also associatively, by speculating about the patient's psychic functioning, in the 'putting oneself into their shoes' sort of way which often frees the supervisee to admit to a block or blind spot in themselves. The latter can become a therapeutic experience for the supervisee and/or the supervisor, as this freeing equals the dropping of a defence, the spontaneous regression that precedes an experience of learning and of psychic change, a moment of truth. For the therapy it means that a step forward in the therapist can lead to a mutative development in the patient – therapist relationship and if the insight can be maintained and taken into the next therapy session it may release fresh material of memories and associations and lead to deeper psychic levels. We have all had the experience of a good hour in supervision being followed by a good hour in therapy when the patient talks and behaves as if he had been a fly on the wall during the supervision.These examples of an unconscious communication from the well-supervised therapist to the patient vindicate the imperative for supervision, though they usually cannot be proved or made statistically significant for research purposes.

The well-timed supervisory intervention can become a model for the well-timed therapeutic interpretation. This statement can be reversed to read 'the badly timed supervisory intervention can have adverse effects on the therapy'. Supervisees tell us when something we have suggested doesn't work more often than when it does. This is understandable: we all tend to take the credit for good work and blame others for failures, unless, of course, one is of the self-denigratory sort that magnifies their own presumed faults in order to get constant attention and support. I personally try to refrain from telling people what to do, because it gets distorted in the translation from one situation to another. On the other hand, I find it useful to speculate what I might have said if I had been there, in an experimental sort of way which carries no obligation to imitate. Speculation can be a waste of time when it becomes an end in itself, a game of scoring degrees of cleverness. But it can also be a rehearsal, a trying out of alternatives and possibilities, a flexing of one's therapeutic muscles, a practising of the repertoire and an oiling of the machine that needs to be in good running order to respond to the unpredictable challenges of our work.

Supervision can be seen as a learning from experience, a learning by doing. Apart from the sequence of trial and error that characterises much of early learning, which is the basis of the scientific method and of the struggle for existence, there is a sequence of four steps that can be observed in supervision (as in other adult learning situations), when the telling of an actual experience is followed by the stage of reflection which leads to the stage of understanding from which experimenting and action become possible. The supervisor is alongside the therapist/learner as observer/reflector/meaning-maker and experimenter, while the doing, i.e., the experiencing and acting, constitutes the therapist's practice. When I spoke of 'vertical time' I meant the time of the individual session in which this cycle of experiential learning runs its inevitable course from one stage to the next, though not always as neatly as in the model described. The supervisor and supervision is the container in which the chemistry of this process happens more or less safely, but it is important to attend to the structure so that each phase gets enough time for maximum effectiveness. When there is too much telling of the story the reflection and meaning-making is curtailed which then cripples the experimenting and preparation for further action, and leaves no time for an analysis of the overall dynamic or for summarising.

The latter, like summarising in therapy, is a practice that varies enormously among individual practitioners, from the lengthy and comprehensive session overview to the laconic 'time is up'. It depends on the stage of the learner as much as on the supervisor's skills and their need to be systematic or authoritative. It is an essential part of the containing that supervision offers to the anxious, uncertain and heavily laden supervisee, but it may also reflect an anxiety on the part of the supervisor, and be a defence against uncertainty and not-knowing. Another element of the cycle that needs to be watched is the performance anxiety or performance style of the participants: the brilliant presenter and the brilliant conceptualiser are equally suspect as they may be defending against exposure or competition and hence avoiding the mutuality of the task, which is to understand the patient, not to impress or shine. Timing and structuring go hand in hand in this learning from experience where the learner is accompanied in their practising attentively and meticulously like the apprentice is by the master craftsman. Teaching a child to ride a bicycle requires similar intuition and facilitation on the part of the parent who holds on to the saddle until the cyclist appears to be steady and going straight, and still gives a helping hand around a bend in the road until that task is also managed. Yet there are frequent falls for the beginner that require picking up, bandaging, detraumatising, and even experienced cyclists need training and coaching until they can be trusted onto the open road. And there is so much more to learn for the therapist.

Time and memory

Question: How do busy supervisors cope with the mass of material, persons, names, incidents, feelings and projections that they are presented with and how do their memories store and retrieve information as necessary? Freud (1912) goes at length into this question and comes up with the notion of 'evenly suspended attention' which allows the memory to register and retain masses of material in a free-associative kind of way, while suspending expectations and judgement.

Bion's (1962) statement 'without memory and desire' deals similarly with the therapist's (and, by analogy, the supervisor's) memory problem by leaving its functioning to the unconscious, as Freud had recommended. Instead of memorising detail in the way of a model schoolchild, we should learn to trust our memories to throw up the relevant information by association, like a computer at the click of the mouse. If they don't, then examine the resistance, i.e. trust your memory to be meaningful in the overall context of the therapy or supervision. But as with the computer there can be such things as psychic overload, crossed wires, or free associations leading you up the garden path, and the more patients or supervisees you have the more likely it is that things get filed away into the wrong drawers. I have heard of a new condition called 'information fatigue syndrome' and sometimes I think the diagnosis fits the supervisor when the many people in his or her head begin to jostle and get mixed up in an uncomfortable way which indicates that there may be more than enough of them claiming the limited space and capacity of his or her memory.

The trouble with supervision is that everything is in multiples of two as supervisees and patients need to be stored together, and some of the more experienced supervisees can have over ten cases. Even weekly supervision does not necessarily deal with a situation where every supervisee expects you to remember their cases as if they were your own and needs to be reminded that without a short introduction the supervisor's computer memory won't be able to throw up the right person. 'Remember such and such . . .' they say and launch into a presentation that assumes powers of total recall. I usually stop them straight away with the remark 'remind me . . .', or I let them go on for a while in the hope that some trigger will open the relevant file in my mind, which, remarkably, usually works. It certainly helps when somebody says, 'let me jog your memory a little' or when they preface their presentation with a thumbnail sketch of the patient and where they have got to with him or her.

But what I really prefer is a profile of each patient which I use as an *aide-mémoire* during the presentation and which miraculously turns into an Ariadne's thread, guiding me into, around and out of the maze of each individual life story, a template into which I fit the detail of the presentation and usually I soon enough find my bearings. It is a method that became necessary with an increasing supervisory workload and it has served me well, with a few exceptions when the ongoing therapy had unearthed major life events and pathology not mentioned in the profile. Maybe the thumbnail sketch is no more than a talisman, a transitional object that gives me the confidence to hand myself over to the presentation unafraid, trusting that my memory will not let me down when I need to remember something urgently and spontaneously.

I don't regularly take copious notes to consult. There would be so much more to read and I usually do not know which patient a supervisee is going to bring unless there is only one case under supervision. Also, and there I agree wholeheartedly with Bion, it is much better not to bring in knowledge of my own before and during the first bit of the presentation, so as to allow the material to affect me freshly, without bias or foreknowledge, and to give my intuition the chance to get to work on it. Sometimes, I find, the less you know the more you see and hear, and after a while, things come flooding back and fit together as in a puzzle or in a photographic image that builds up a picture sequentially, until it is complete and makes sense. This is particularly interesting in group supervision when different members of a group home in on different bits of the presented material which join together to produce a multifaceted impression of the total situation to which the supervisor may then add the final word, or from which s/he may choose the most meaningful focus. The therapist's and supervisor's selective task is finding the point of maximum pain, identifying the suffering amidst the bric-a-brac of life, thinking the unthinkable.

I have only begun to think of memory in relation to supervisory work, but my hunch is it is as crucial a concept for this task as for the writing of history and of memoirs. We are, after all, dealing with people's histories, with their narratives constructed and reconstructed in therapy in order for them to make sense out of the chaos of their individual lives which have gone wrong and become stuck, painful and meaningless. Proust's (1981) description of the associative functioning of memory for the linking of past and present is a useful pointer to what happens in therapy and in supervision when an interpretation or intervention is made, by allowing it to happen by free association, which becomes the intuitive trigger of painful memories for the patient. It is important to access these memories at the right moment and to provide a therapeutic or supervisory context in which they can be used creatively. The secret lies in the ability to free associate, to reflect on and to process what has been found by this method.

I am still uncertain about the extent to which therapeutic practice sharpens (or blunts) one's powers of recall, about the secret of timing, the availability of stored memories and the methods of selecting therapeutically-significant information from one's memory.

Ending supervision

Much care is usually taken when supervision begins and much has been said and written about the supervisory contract. 'In the beginning is my end', as the poet T.S. Eliot says, which indicates that many a good or bad ending can be traced back to what happened; what was done or not done right at the beginning. But how about the ending itself? Do we still too readily assume that in supervision the ending will take care of itself rather than need to be anticipated and prepared for as in therapy? I don't think so, because increasingly, certainly in training, there are rites and procedures to address issues of endings well before the actual cut-off point to allow anxieties related to previous endings and losses to be aired and worked on. We now know that it is necessary to understand the affective problems of learning and the important part played by issues of attachment and separation in the learning relationship, as well as its inevitable transference ingredients.

As supervision straddles the gap between education and therapy (which is one of the central themes of this book) it sets in motion its own complex emotional mechanisms when it ends, whether planned or unplanned, mutual, agreed or anticipated. The presence of clients and patients plays a further complicating part, whether they carry on with the supervisee (but are lost to the supervisor) or finish at the same time (and are lost to both participants). It may be too early or too late, for one or the other of the participants, and in both situations there will inevitably be regret, anger or blaming. There are always things which have never been said and cannot now be said, about loving or hating feelings, about hurtful remarks, opportunities missed, methods disliked, expectations unfulfilled and sometimes the ending will sharpen a sense of 'if only we had done this or that' particularly in the areas of praise, honesty or respect.

When the ending is initiated by one of the supervisory partners, and not mutually, there may remain an air of betrayal, resentment, and rejection, leaving unspoken questions like: why now and who will I be replaced by? Because of this fear of hurting or being hurt (am I good enough, are you good enough?) supervision among consenting partners (i.e. not in training) often goes on for too long and evidence of this may be found in the stagnating or declining quality of the supervisee's clinical work. Can patients prosper when therapists are unable to decide whether or not to carry on with their supervisor, who may have gone stale on them or become bored with them? A cut-off point would be the moment when the supervisee and/or the supervisor find themselves having fantasies of wanting a different supervisor or wishing to be without the supervisee, which may be due to natural ambivalence, attrition, or yearning for something new, all of which is difficult to address in supervision, unless a patient's clinical material is interpreted as a reflection process.

It is not surprising that an ending in private supervision is often more difficult to initiate when there is a positive transference to the supervisor with whom the weekly meeting has assumed the nature of a cherished routine and where a plateau of colleagueship has been reached that is creative and nourishing. Who then depends on whom, who is nourished by whom and who is learning more? In these situations the training supervisor, in particular, can feel the wrench like the parent who has to let go of a child whose growing into adulthood has been rewarding to watch, and who will be sorely missed for the weekly instalments of narcissistic gratification and intellectual stimulation.

When there is a negative transference, there may remain loose ends of anger, frustration, narcissistic injury and pain which can go on haunting the participants and complicate the mourning with unresolved grievances and regrets, self-justification and rationalisation, due to all the unsaid things which have been eating away at the participants and would, of course, form the bedrock of working through in a therapeutic relationship. Resolving the transference is not one of the supervisory tasks.

The ending of a supervisory relationship thus requires an emotional maturity (and therefore a degree of self-awareness and courage) that enables the participants to end for practical reasons when their emotional needs for and transference issues with each other cannot be analysed and fulfilled because the focus of their relationship was to do with the emotional needs and issues of the patient. As supervision is a continuing professional necessity for the practitioner who needs to move on in order to develop further and to find another person to learn from, the supervisor is like the teacher who has to be able to let go generously and to respect the learning needs of the pupils, to watch them outgrow him/her and to engage legitimately with other colleagues, while the aim of the therapist is to enable the patient to do without him/her and ideally not to need another therapist, certainly not immediately.

As with the contract made at the beginning of supervision, the ending of it entails careful attention to such practical issues as responsibility for patients and future plans, ongoing learning needs and assessment of progress; also in relation to strengthening the 'internal supervisor', mutual feedback, issues of paperwork and requests for references. There may be verbal acknowledgement and recognition of the attainment of colleagueship and of all this might entail in terms of boundaries, future socialising, working together, meeting (and greeting) each other at professional or cultural events.

The ending of supervision, as the beginning of it, needs to be a professional rite of passage in order to become meaningful as an emotional stage and transition, and to highlight the important relationship aspect of the supervisory experience. Then, the supervisor can become internalised and take his or her place in the supervisee's internal world as an internal good object, an ongoing influence and a model on which to draw.

I have concentrated on the individual supervision relationship which always embraces the patient(s), to become triadic. When supervision is done in groups (whether peer or supervisor-led) the issue of ending is complicated by the numbers involved, by unconscious group dynamics and unconscious needs for sharing and choosing. Either the whole group will end and need time to dissolve the matrix, or individuals (supervisor or supervisees) will leave the group and create a gap for each group member and the group as a whole. The complexities of leavetaking in the group are multiplied by the leaving members' patients and by the consequent reshuffle of alliances and subgoups, until a new group identity (including new group supervisor and new group members) can emerge from the mourning and working-through process. Trainee supervision groups, in my experience, usually develop their own ending rituals with the help of gifts to the supervisor or of a shared farewell meal in which the atmosphere of social intercourse prevents feared disintegration and ushers in the separation and mourning processes which will continue beyond the actual ending of the last group session until they, too, fade away, leaving behind the group as an internal good object, if it had been truly functional as a supervision group.

One very important supervisory task is the assessment of the supervisee's clinical work and this will be regular or ongoing depending on the context and on the professional stage the supervisee has reached. Whether the work is done in training or in private practice, in a charitable agency or a statutory clinic the supervisor's monitoring function in relation to the patient's welfare and to the supervisee's professional attitude is an essential ingredient of a task which may include clinical responsibility for the supervisee's cases and accountability for the patients' handling and progress in an organisation. In situations where the supervisor is dissatisfied or worried about a supervisee's professional functioning and where the supervisor may have to take steps to warn, to discontinue or even to suspend the supervisee from work or from his or her training there will be an ending to supervision that is difficult to bring about amicably. The supervisor will have to be clear about the criteria s/he is applying and will have to consider the supervisee's welfare as well as the patient's, to analyse his or her unconscious motives and the objective reasons for taking the drastic decision of withdrawing his or her support and his or her imprimatur from the supervisee.

The most obvious example would be a supervisee who is over-identified with his or her patients to the point of dangerous enmeshment in their pathology which prevents him/her from thinking clearly about the patient's clinical material, from formulating meaningful interpretations and from making interventions which help the patient to a better understanding of his or her internal world. Another example is the supervisee who is incapable of understanding the interpersonal processes in the therapeutic relationship in terms of their transferential and counter-transferential implications and hence misses the significant psychodynamic cues which underlie and explain the patient's projective and introjective defences against his or her unconscious conflicts. If this 'subjective' attitude or this lack of analytic processing and understanding is observed in more than one case over a substantial period of time and appears to be a general inability to be helpfully empathic as well as creatively interactive the supervisor will have to grasp the nettle and inform the supervisee of their serious concern regarding the supervisee's clinical work, indicating that something radical needs to be done to protect the patient from further exposure to the supervisee's fumbling ministrations.

At best there may ensue a discussion about the supervisor's particular reservations and clearly spelt out reasons for recommending that the supervisee stop working and training, either temporarily, if they suffer from burn-out, preoccupation with personal difficulties, or from an excess of blind spots and dumb spots still amenable to further training and/or therapy. Or for good, which would be the worst scenario. In the latter case there might be an apodictic 'no' to the supervisee's continuation of therapeutic work and an irrevocable decision to end their supervision together with the termination of the supervisee's clinical practice. In both cases the supervisee may comply with the outcome, though not necessarily because s/he accepts the verdict but more likely because s/he decides to submit to the supervisor's authority and power. Or s/he may decide to appeal against and reject the supervisor's verdict, reading it as hostility or as a wilfully punitive attitude, in order not to have to face the humiliating admission of failure and loss of self esteem.

On one rare occasion when a supervisee admitted to me that 'she would not have respected me if I had allowed her to pass', I realised that the scrupulous exposure of a narcissistic confidence trickster is as necessary for the conscientious supervisor to carry out as is the careful explaining to an incompetent counsellor that they simply haven't got what it takes to do the work. It is part of the difficult ethics of supervision to stop the impostors, the badly trained, the insufficiently analysed, the unaware, the ignorant and the unscrupulous practitioners from calling themselves therapists and from practising the complex and responsible art of healing when they are a danger to patients and are able to do harm to them.

To end supervision on that harsh note is impossibly difficult and the only hope is that the affected supervisees may realise one day that it was necessary and probably even caring to stop them from being a danger to themselves and to others, and that in the long run, they had to be prevented from doing work to which they weren't suited or gifted. Then the end of supervision will be experienced as an act of professional integrity, as the inevitable conclusion of a false choice rather than as a sadistic rejection or brutal exclusion from practising a desired profession, as it may have been experienced at the time.

References

Bion, W.R. (1962) *Learning from Experience*. London: Maresfield Reprints.
Freud, S. (1912) *Recommendations to the Doctor Regarding Psychoanalytic Treatment*, Standard Edition, 12. London: Hogarth Press.
Proust, M. (1981) *Remembrance of Things Past*. Harmondsworth: Penguin.
Strachey, J. (1934) 'The nature of the therapeutic action of psychoanalysis', *International Journal of Psychoanalysis*, 15: 127–159.

Index